Black Thighs
Black Guys
&
Bedroom Lies

To Earth,
  I am so glad I met you.
This marks the beginning of a
wonderful relationship.

Black Thighs
Black Guys
&
Bedroom Lies

HASANI PETTIFORD

HASANI PETTIFORD PUBLICATIONS
West Orange, New Jersey

Hasani Pettiford is available for speaking engagements.
Contact office or send email to info@renmanserv.com

Black Thighs, Black Guys & Bedroom Lies

Cover Design by:
Vizuri Graphics – Danielle Pettiford

Editor:
Shirley Pettiford

ISBN: 0-9707915-0-X

For booking information contact:
Renaissance Management Services
P.O. Box 548
New York, NY 10031
Phone (866) 317-5550 * Fax (212) 368-5228
www.hasani.com

Discounts on this book are available for bulk purchases.
Write or call for information on our discount program.

Contents

Acknowledgments

*B*lack Thighs, Black Guys & Bedroom Lies was a very difficult book to write. It forced me to re-evaluate my relationship with myself, with my God and with all those around me. For a year, I was called to a life of continuous prayer, fasting and consecration. In that time, I hid, cried and struggled with past issues. But through that purging process, my misery ultimately became my ministry. Thus, *Black Thighs, Black Guys & Bedroom Lies* was born. This book has truly revolutionized my life, and my prayer is that it will revolutionize yours as well.

To my parents, Ralph and Shirley Pettiford: This book would not exist today if not for the seed that you both have planted in my heart. Proverbs 22:6 says, "Train up a child in the way he should go: and when he is old, he will not depart from it." My dwelling place of the past 24 years has served as an oasis of innovative and entrepreneurial pursuits. From Pettiford Signs & Graphics, to Popular Club and Avon, your workings have sparked a desire within me to discover my own hopes and dreams. From your foundation, this book was birthed.

To my spiritual father, Pastor Paul Dean: Your guidance and genuine friendship have transformed my life. Your life example is a testament that, with God, all things are possible. You have truly inspired me to go M.A.D. (make a difference) with this book.

To Danielle Thomas: You have been my number one supporter from the beginning of this project. Your words of encouragement and edification have elevated me to heights I once thought were unreachable.

A special thanks to Vanessa Foster, Nakeisha McCain, Dimitri Henderson, Dr. Maurice Henderson, Kimcosla Chambers, Shanelle Henry, Aziza Nicholson, Steve Fingal, Renita Oglesby, Asukile Allrich, Tracey Lynn Counts, Novella Dorsey, Robin Clarke, and Derrick Peynado for being very instrumental in bringing this book into existence.

Forward

I am elated *Black Thighs, Black Guys & Bedroom Lies* was written. It is an eye opener for everyone. Hasani Pettiford has revealed that it's not all right to hop from bed to bed, or to slip and slid between the sheets. He has informed us that, no matter how good it feels to the flesh, it's the mind and soul that suffer thereafter. I believe that every Pastor, Preacher, Evangelist and Minister should read this book. Don't read it to preach it; don't read it to teach it; don't even read it to save others. Read this book to save yourselves from this sex plight that has devoured so many of our lives.

Hasani Pettiford has taken a stand that many have been afraid to take. This book has exposed, revealed and uncovered what God has intended for pleasure between a Husband and a Wife and the divine behavior of singles. This book is a wake-up call for all. Just take a look around you. Many relationships have been broken and destroyed because of an uncontrollable passion overriding what is right. Ask yourself, "Have I been caught in this trade wind?" This book will cause females to ask themselves, "Does he really want me or does he just want my body?" Brothers will also realize through this profound Masterpiece that they can't continue to play and swing with women's hearts and emotions, that it's time to come out of the playground and into the Captains seat and lead our women into the hands of God and not into our Beds.

Due to the material in this book, I advise a **"Reader's Caution."**
Caution:
1. This book will dissolve many relationships.
2. This book will cause many women to put men out of their beds.
3. This book will raise questions you never once thought to ask.
4. This book will make you scream "No More – Time Out – It's All Or Nothing."

5. This book is the Truth, the whole Truth and nothing but the Truth. And, if you're not ready for the truth, then you're not ready for this book. And if you're not ready to read this book, then you're not ready to be free. Because the Truth will make you free. Why be bound? Read and be free: spiritually, emotionally and physically.
6. Last. This book will cause tears to roll, hearts to hurt and hard decisions to be made. However, the author does not leave you hopeless. He articulates a hope in God, Who is a mender of broken hearts.

Black Thighs, Black Guys & Bedroom Lies counteracts what is perpetuated throughout the media: Get sex, get sex and get more sex. A bumper sticker once read "Got sex?" Its message was simple. "I'm looking for some and, if you're willing to give it up then I'll take it." People are walking around looking for sex like a lost puppy looking for shelter. But thank God for Hasani Pettiford who has let us know – that if you've got your hands out ready to catch it – you're going to catch a lot of other things right along with it. And it doesn't matter whether you wear a "Glove" or not. Hasani clearly lets us know that no matter what the media says. Brothers, the next time you go to "put it in", make sure God is in it. Ladies, the next time you "open it up", make sure Heaven is opening up with you. If not, then it's not right. And if you don't know, now you know.

Even though this book is entitled *Black Thighs, Black Guys & Bedroom Lies*. I believe in my heart that it will do much justice for White thighs, White guys, Hispanic thighs, Hispanic guys, etcetera. This book is for everybody who's somebody. It's not limited to a particular race. This book was designed to wake up a nation. So get ready, and take off your criticism hat and put on your receiving helmet because anybody who's somebody will gain insight from this phenomenal book, *Black Thighs, Black Guys & Bedroom Lies.* Grace and Peace.

Pastor Paul Dean
Visions of God Family Worship

Why Black Thighs,
Black Guys & Bedroom Lies?

Why Black Thighs, Black Guys & Bedroom Lies?
Because according to a report issued by the Children's Defense Fund, fewer than 20 percent of young adults remain virgins throughout their teenage years. Every 65 seconds a black teenager becomes sexually active. Every 104 seconds a black teenage girl becomes pregnant. Every 20 hours a black child or young adult under the age of 23 dies from causes related to HIV.

Why Black Thighs, Black Guys & Bedroom Lies?
Because the Black family structure has been destroyed. According to the *Baltimore Sun*, approximately 66 percent of all Black marriages end in divorce. As a result, over ten million children under eighteen have parents who are divorced or separated. Single parents run almost 80 percent of the households.

Why Black Thighs, Black Guys & Bedroom Lies?
Because Blacks are 30 times more likely to be infected with a sexually transmitted disease than their white counterpart. According to a special report done by Ebony Magazine, AIDS is the number one killer of Blacks under the age of 55. Even though Blacks are only 12 percent of the population, they account for 45 percent of all reported AIDS cases in the United States. Black females account for a whopping 60 percent of all American women with the disease. The Center for Disease Control (CDC) reports nearly 100 new cases of AIDS among Blacks every day.

Why Black Thighs, Black Guys & Bedroom Lies?
Because too many people have fallen victim to looking for love in all the wrong places and getting into relationships for all the wrong reasons. As a result, many men and women are bound up, carrying baggage from past relationships and sexual encounters.

Why Black Thighs, Black Guys & Bedroom Lies?

To convey one simple message: "Walk in the Spirit and ye shall not fulfill the lust of the flesh...Now the works of the flesh are manifest, which are these; Adultery, fornication, uncleanness, lasciviousness...I have also told you in time past, that they which do such things shall not inherit the kingdom of God."

Galatians 5:16-21

Why Black Thighs, Black Guys & Bedroom Lies?

I wrote this book to expose all of the sexual games and bedroom lies played that often result in destroyed relationships between Black men and women. This book is audacious enough to charter grounds many have not explored. It is bound to leave the cognizant nodding their heads and the unknowing speechless. Therefore, I promise to leave no stone unturned. So, if you are looking for a *Sesame Street* approach to relationships, this is not the book for you. But, if you are ready for a punch-you-in-the-throat, hard-hitting approach to sex and relationships, then keep reading. This book will change your life forever. So, buckle up as I take you on a journey through *Black Thighs, Black Guys & Bedroom Lies.*

Black Thighs

As you enter into my temple
A new world begins
A connection that causes an infection
Of deep wounds, scarred hearts and burned souls
Am I out of control
To think that it could be, Eternity
As I look upon your face
An image staring back at me
Reflects so vividly
My dreams, wants, needs
And a desire to be pleased
I must fall down on my knees
And pray that I am forgiven for this act of sin
That started from within
Cuz my soul cries out for more
But this physical attraction
Has become a distraction
For me to see a world of indecent proposals
Between black thighs, black guys and bedroom lies
One by one, a piece of me taken
By this man and that man
Left drained and ashamed
From the bondage of my pain
In the end what shall this be
To lose a piece of my strength
Or to gain another man's spirit?

Black Thighs Black Guys & Bedroom Lies

Chapter One

THE GAME

Six feet two inches of man sculpted from black onyx. Weighing a meaty 220 pounds of muscle. His biceps, triceps, chest, and washboard stomach similar to that of Tyson Beckford. His penetrating eyes could put any woman in a trance. His sultry voice could soothe a savage beast. His almost blinding white teeth could illuminate a dimly lit room. His strong hands showed hard labor, yet they were made pleasurable for a silky massage. Pharaoh was definitely all man.

He drives a sleek metallic silver 430 CLK Mercedes Benz with a built-in navigational system, Coach leather interior seats, and a twenty-disk CD changer. One glance at his dangling car keys would attract the attention of any woman that appreciates the finer things in life.

Very meticulous about his physical appearance, Pharaoh wore only the best. His dress was replete with an Armani suit, Georgio Brutini snakeskin shoes, accented with a Luigi Borrelli custom made shirt, a Sulka tie, Versace glasses, a Dolce and Gabbana belt, and a Cartier solid steel watch. For Pharaoh, platinum was not an option, it was rather a necessity.

Pharaoh was a seasoned fitness instructor and personal trainer for pre-Olympiad athletes. Unfortunately, a knee injury ruined his chances of qualifying for the '98 Summer Games. It was at that critical moment that he swore that if he couldn't make it to the Olympics, he would spend the rest of his days training others to go in his place. Though his profession had definitely raised a few eyebrows, what enticed women most about Pharaoh was his appreciation for fine arts. Pharaoh's passion was photography. He had a modest studio set-up inside his luxurious Upper-Manhattan apartment overlooking the Hudson River.

But, what Pharaoh loved more than photography was women. And his camera was the device that was surreptitiously used to reel in any woman who would succumb to his bait. Some men took pride in their personal coin or stamp collection. However, Pharaoh was a collector of women. In his darkroom hung the pictures of all of the women whom he had engaged in sporadic sexual affairs. To no surprise, this was the one room that was off limits to all of his carefully hand picked guests.

One thing that Pharaoh did not do was discriminate. "Women are women!", he adamantly stated to Steve, an old classmate of his. " If she has a pretty face, nice body and is willing to give up the panties at the drop of a dime, she qualifies in my book. As a matter of fact, I'm looking for a new model-type to add to my collection."

His obsession to find this woman took him on a sexual stakeout through nightclubs, beauty salons, black professional meetings, and even churches. Well, after nights of an exhausting search, Pharaoh decided to spend Friday night having drinks with a couple of friends at a Mid-Manhattan social club called Nell's.

With no intention of meeting anyone, there she stood— perfection in a tantalizing casing. Tall, thin and lithe like a dancer. She wore a 36' 24' 36' frame and possessed the kind of beauty that

18

could make a blind man blush. She had a soft, mahogany complexion, deep, oval-shaped, chestnut brown eyes, and her hair—ooh. Her hair was not long and flowing in the wind. It was a sandy brown, soft wavy natural.

She wore a tightly fit BCBG low-cut chemise, slightly revealing her ballerina shoe tattoo perfectly placed on the innermost part of her breast. And as his eyes made their way down her body, he took a liking to her sheer white Chanel matching bottom, which exposed the outline of her Victoria Secret lingerie.

But the best was yet to come: buttressing this beauty were the feet of a goddess. Feet that could not just be placed in any shoe. But a work of flawlessness which was appropriately showcased in a sexy sling back, open-toe pump with a stiletto heel. And her body was silently endorsed with the sweet fragrance of romance, a smell that lingered with the stride of every step. Her step of confidence could grab the attention of any innocent bystander, instantly making them victim to her most alluring existence.

If she dare open her mouth, she would leave men spellbound by her soft and tranquil voice. And as the tide of an ocean departs from its shore, so does every word that flows from her mouth. Indigo was, indeed, a phenomenal woman.

Without hesitation, Pharaoh immediately approached her. To snare this beauty, he had to come with something completely off the cuff. So, he confidently slid his way into a conversation with her, knowing that he had the power to talk a woman right out of her clothes. The sexual attraction between them was apparent. Well, twenty minutes and three drinks later, their minds began to take them in different directions. As they spoke, while carefully focusing on her body, he fantasized what sex would be like with her. Is she a freak or is she conservative? Is she willing to try new things? Will she expect me to call her when it's all over? While focusing on his conversation, Indigo fantasized what it would be like to be his woman. Is he married? Well, who cares! What kind of job does he have? Uuuuhhh, I wonder what he looks like underneath those clothes? Eventually parting with questions unanswered, they left each other with a titillating thirst of curiosity eagerly waiting to be quenched.

Three weeks and two days later, Pharoah and Indigo reunited for their fourth meeting. After exhausting all of the possibilities of what to do, they both agreed that his apartment would be appropriate. Besides, it's been a whole three weeks. "I'm gonna know as much as I'm gonna know about this man," Indigo thought to herself.

Pharaoh coaxed Indigo into bringing an extra pair of clothing for a personal photo shoot that he had been so eagerly awaiting. Indigo willingly agreed because she knew that one glance of her in the right dress would be too much for him to handle. And the minute she stepped into the apartment, it was on. Lights, camera and a whole lot of action!

Indigo knew before she arrived that she would be serving a full course sexual meal. After a few drinks and light conversation, Indigo decided to slip into something more comfortable. With her clothes draped over a small Venetian screen, carefully placed at the far-end of the room, she slipped into her outfit. As she emerged from behind the screen, she approached the camera wearing a long sheer floral gown, revealing what was underneath. The gown had thin spaghetti straps that crossed in the back, and a front slit showing the soft skin of her inner thigh. "Are you ready, baby?" Pharaoh confidently asked. Before she could respond, the sounds of a winding camera and the flashing of bright lights began to fill the room.

With Maxwell's song, *Woman's Work*, gently playing in the background she began to dance to the music. With the stride of every step and the shift of every pose, her body began to speak to the camera. Without hesitation, the camera would respond with the reply, "Snap!" Gracefully flowing like a ballerina dancer, the camera caught every expression of detail. "Snap! Snap! Snap!" said the camera to her partially covered body.

Approaching the end of his fifth roll of film, to Indigo's delight, Pharaoh stepped in front of the camera and proceeded to finish what she had started. What Indigo initially offered as an erotic appetizer, with just one touch, became a full-course meal. They began to relive the chapters of one of the most romantic love novels. And, as he penetrated into her walls of suspicion Indigo felt a bolt of lightening energy shoot from her womb straight to her heart. Though he dwelled within her lower region, simultaneously, her heart was electrically massaged and stimulated.

It was at that moment that Indigo exhaled. What she felt wasn't love, but it was what she was longing for, for quite some time. It was a feeling of complete gratification. The ability to be herself, without feeling belittled by other men for her insatiable desire for sex. The sexual experiences of her past were stale and trite, but Pharaoh possessed something that was just unexplainable. It defied description. "Wow, he has good looks. He's very successful and he has the kind of sex to keep me happy for days. With a combination like that, what woman wouldn't want a man like this for the rest of her life?" Indigo thought to herself as she incessantly stared at him. She caught the "jones" and there was no turning back.

As they lay there finding solace in each other's embrace, Indigo comfortably said, "I can get used to this." Immediately alarmed by such a statement, Pharaoh quickly responded. "What, what do you mean?" he stuttered. "What I mean is, I really like this and I like you, and I like what we have. Don't you?" "Uh, I mean, I like you too baby but let's just enjoy the moment, o.k." "Fine", Indigo hesitantly responded.

A week later, Indigo wanted to see him again and arranged for another rendezvous, but Pharaoh never showed up. Concerned about his whereabouts, Indigo called his home, but all she got was his answering machine. Though she only left one message, her number showed up on Pharaoh's caller I.D. six times. Three days later Pharaoh called and apologized for not showing.

"I'm sorry baby, but I had some new clients to attend to and our date just slipped my mind." "Well, when am I gonna see you?" Indigo impatiently asked. "Look, I have a four-week training camp up in the Catskills and I'm leaving in two days. I'm busy running, trying to get things in order before I leave. Listen, I know this may seem abrupt, but that's how the business is. I don't work on a time clock. When the opportunity presents itself, I have to run with it. You understand, don't you?" Pharaoh nonchalantly asks. A dead silence fills the air. The tension is so thick that you can cut it with a knife. "Look, I'll call you when I get back." Without so much as a goodbye, Pharaoh swiftly hangs up the phone. With the dial tone buzzing in her ear, Indigo cannot bring herself to put down the phone.

All of a sudden, a nauseous sensation begins to overwhelm her. All of the blood in her body races to her head. Her heart is throbbing excessively. Every thought, feeling and emotion saturates her mind. Frozen in her seat with no thought of what to do next, tears of resentment slowly begin to cascade down her face. Her upper lip quivers with disgust about what has just occurred. Everything, all of a sudden, appears blurry and the room begins to spin in circles. Indigo is now detached from reality. She spends the next three hours staring at the swinging brass pendulum hanging from her grandfather clock.

Meanwhile, Pharaoh applauds himself on a job well done, as he ponders which photograph of Indigo to hang along his infamous wall of fame. Starring at an array of perfectly pinned-up playmates, Pharaoh stands in complete amazement of his accomplishments.

Soap Opera, right? Wrong! Another one of Hollywood's twisted and sordid love stories turned sour? Not quite. This is just another classic example of what takes place when traveling down the dark tunnel of lover's lane. It is a game full of lies, money, deception, resentment, strife, and a whole lot of sex. It is a world that has left many Black men and women at war with one another. A war of open-armed sexual conflict, replete with antagonism and contention. A war that has left many Black women sexually exploited, emotionally wounded, vengeful, pregnant, abandoned and even homeless by Black men who refuse to acknowledge the error of their ways. At the same time, many Black men have been emasculated, vilified, emotionally callous, and even financially broke by the malice of scandalous Black women. As each day goes by, the relational state of affairs gets progressively worse. Why? It's simple! The very games that have been performed on the courts, rings, and fields of our society, for our own personal pleasure and delight, have crept into the most intimate and sacred settings of our lives.

The Game Overview

In order to understand what has taken place in the lives of many Black men and women, it is important to understand the similarities between sports games and sexual games played in relationships. When Michael Jordan scores a game-winning shot; when Ken Griffey Jr. effortlessly knocks a ball out of the park, or when Tiger Woods hits a hole in one we instinctively applaud their efforts. They are often praised for all of their accomplishments. Many athletes often become heroes. Sports and games have become American pastimes that have helped shape the cultural identity of this nation. They are activities that are fun, yet their concept that is very simple.

A game is a competitive activity in which two or more rivals contend with one another for a level of superiority or victory. It is often an organized program or contest comprised of strategies, a point system to properly determine a winner, and a host of rules to govern the activity of its participants in order to ensure honorable play. At the end of each game a winner is declared. So, one triumphs at the expense of another's loss. Seems pretty fair, right? Sure it does. However, once this game concept is brought into the confines of a relationship, all hell is bound to break lose.

Relationships were designed to function in a cooperative, not a competitive arena. It is an institution where two people are committed to working together to produce results that are best for all parties involved. It is a process of thoroughly understanding issues and resolving them in a mutually beneficial way. Such interaction seeks to produce a win/win outcome.

However, the sexual games played by both men and women inevitably create a lose/lose situation. These games are often destructive to both present and future relationships. This destructiveness is why players cannot properly function in relationships. 'Playas' normally wind up in connections. Maulana Karenga, professor and author, coined the term 'Connection.' There are flesh connections, cash connections and dependency connections. A connection represents an individual who is tied to another for very specific reasons. I'm sure that we can all conjure

23

up an incalculable number of connections that exist. However, the objective of this chapter is to delve into the intricacies of the flesh/cash connection.

In order for the game to begin, the player must identify the goal. The individual is often not the prize. However, it is acquiring what that individual has access to that becomes the reward. For instance, male players see women as objects that perform a specific function: sex. Male players want women for their bodies and the power they feel from the thrill of the conquest. They are likely to seek women who they find beautiful and sexy. Women 'playas', on the other hand, see men as a way of obtaining a particular lifestyle they want. Many are status seekers, freeloaders, or women looking for an easy ride (both financially and sexually). Note: Many women crave sex just as much as men do, and are relentless in their pursuit. They seek men who have what they want and then drain them of their resources. These women will bounce from man to man until they find one who falls for their scheme.

So, while men crave vagina, women crave penis and possessions. In this warped scenario the bedroom becomes the marketplace and the bed becomes the bartering table from which all transactions are made. Occasionally, when the product is as good as the presentation, everyone's happy. However, these types of arrangements often turn sour, leaving the other with a raw deal. Why? This game is played under false pretenses. Therefore, satisfaction is never guaranteed. You play at your own risk.

It's a game of winner takes all. Either you play or get played. The rules of engagement are simple. There are no rules. No guidelines. No sideline referees monitoring fair play. No flagrant fouls, illegal defense plays or personal penalties. There is a 'whatever it takes' mentality. In this game, every player plays for keeps and only the strongest survive. The player's creed is simple: 'Nobody gets attached, nobody gets hurt' and 'all is fair in lust and war.' Such a philosophy requires an emotional numbness that detaches the player from all feelings. Why? Because of the old adage: Whoever is the most emotionally committed to the relationship has the least power in it.

Now that we have successfully covered the game concept, let's take a closer look at its players.

The Players
The Black Vagina Finda

The male player is otherwise known as, The Black Vagina Finda. He has been crowned with this title because sex is his only goal. He doesn't love women. He doesn't like women. He lusts women. In fact, it's not even women he desires. It's what women have to offer that entices him. Many of his sexual decisions are strictly based on his penis and his erection. He has an overwhelming compulsion to continuously hold his crotch, which reflects his attitude towards life. Such behavior reminds him of his sexual role with women. His penis, no matter how big or small, is ruler thus making him ruler. So, he often winds up using his little head instead of his big head. It's sad that a man will sacrifice his life for an erect penis.

The Black Vagina Find successfully masters dehumanizing women. He has been described as a rebel without a pause. A rebel likened to a roaring lion, walking about, seeking whom he can sexually devour. And, he will stop at nothing to get what he wants. According to Dr. Rosie Milligan's *Satisfying The Black Man Sexually*, "Men have lost their jobs for it; Men have lost their lives for it; Men have left their wives for it; Men have left school for it; Men have gone AWOL from the military for it; All for a little piece of real estate with grass growing on it."

Black Vagina Findas don't seek relationships. Relationships are like kryptonite to a player because they represent commitment. He doesn't understand commitment. All he understands is sex. As a result, he chooses to be physically present but emotionally unavailable. Such a lifestyle gives him the ability to come and go as he pleases, having no one to answer to. If a woman appears to be getting too serious, he steps back. He wants sex but only on his terms. Women who are available on demand are his greatest delight. So, he spreads himself among several women. He will have sex with you on Monday and then sex your sister on Tuesday. How? It is quite simple. Sex has no emotional significance to him. It is merely a recreational sport. The ability to sleep with several women provides him with an unrestrained amount of sexual vigor. The Black Vagina Finda's self-identity is wrapped up in the amount of women he sleeps with. Alluring and sexing many women helps him feel good about himself. One man audaciously explains his philosophy of sex as an extra-curricular activity in Michael Baisden's book *Never Satisfied: Why Men Cheat.*

The Basketball Game
I look at my relationships with women like a game of basketball. I'm the coach and they are the players. The first order of business for the coach is to find a star player, a woman to build the team around. She will be expected to come through under pressure, night in and night out. Her responsibilities will include coming to all practice sessions and scoring on a consistent basis. If she performs up to standards, her contract will be renegotiated and she will be allowed to stay with the team indefinitely. Then you have your two back-up players who are also expected to perform well. They are a very integral part of the team since the starter can't be expected to come through 30 consecutive games, if you know what I mean. Finally, you have your two benchwarmers. Although they may not get much starting time, don't sell them short. In a pressure situation, they will give you everything they've got. Recruiting such a cohesive unit is no easy task. You must be willing to travel all across town to find the perfect combination. That includes wedding receptions, bowling alleys, and even funerals. No place is off limits to a coach who is determined to win...The bottom line is this: I need a solid back-up crew in order to make my life more comfortable and secure. The only question is, What do I call this team? How about the Seattle Standbys, or the Atlanta Alternates? I Just Love This Game!

Millions of men across this nation take on the heartless activity of sexing women with no intention to change because every club, corporate office, women's group, and church pew have desperate women willing to spread their legs without cause or conscience. In fact, a man will sleep with a woman he is not physically attracted to just for sex. Why? A true player will not allow himself to experience a sexual drought by going without sex for too long. So, these women serve no other purpose than to fulfill men's sexual urges. Playas want the kind of women who spend 80% of their time with men having sex and the remaining 20% planning where it will happen next. These women don't require much. They're never introduced to family and friends. They're very seldom taken out on dates. Maybe an occasional bite to eat but nothing extravagant. The only investment men make on these women is in purchasing condoms. There are no bonding sessions, candlelight dinners or romantic vacations. All they share is sex.

By now, the question that many of you may be asking is, "Are women really that gullible and easy?" Frankly, some are extremely easy. Give some women a quarter-pounder with cheese and their legs come flying open. Why? The reasons vary: some women are struggling with insecurities, loneliness, and deep self-esteem issues. Others just have an insatiable desire for sex. Yet, there are many women who aren't so easily swayed, and a two-piece biscuit meal just won't do. Many may be good women looking for a decent man. Unfortunately, they have fallen victim to looking for love in all the wrong places and getting into relationships for all the wrong reasons. As a result, these women are snared into sexual exploitation.

At one time, a player may have been very easy to spot within a crowded room, but things have certainly changed. There is no uniform look for a Black Vagina Finda. They come in all shapes, sizes and disguises. He may be the thugged-out brother on the corner or the investment banker on Wall Street. One never knows. The Black Vagina Finda is a compulsive liar who has mastered the art of insensitivity. He will lie, cheat or do whatever it takes to get women. He will act like a devout Christian for the church going lady. He will be a successful business owner for the seasoned lady physician. He will borrow his friend's Porsche to impress the materialistic lady. He will pretend that his friend's penthouse apartment is his own. He will even have fake business cards.

The Black Vagina Finda will succeed until women begin to see through his game. The following is a condensed list of games that the Black Vagina Finda has mastered, which is found in David Burgest's article, *Sexual Games in Black Male/Female Relations.*

1) *If you dance to the music, you got to pay the piper*
The objective is to create a feeling of indebtedness in the female by making her financially dependent on the man. Therefore, financial favors provided by the man must be reciprocated. It is often accomplished by sexual favors given by the female. The problem with this game is that emotional involvement is completely withdrawn which promotes nothing but a cold and callous sexual business arrangement.

2) *If you love me, you will*
The male attempts to coerce the female partner into sexual explorations. The object of the game is to experience sexual self-gratification at the expense of the wishes and desires of the female partner. The statement offered is 'If you love me, you will', while the genuine female response is 'If you love me, you won't ask'. The male's statement places a selfish twist on the concept of what love really means. Any relationship based upon selfish gain and satisfaction is doomed.

3) *I'm mad (angry)*
The Black male ventures to initiate a fraudulently hostile environment in order to justifiably retreat from the relationship based upon his own personal ulterior motives. Normally, the male will resort to such devious antics, in order to escape becoming intimate with another female. After the dirty deed is done, contact with the partner is once again initiated with attempts to mend the relationship.

4) *I just wanna or let me just…*
The Black male successfully deceives the female by saying 'I just want to touch, look, hold, be near or kiss you' when in reality he is seeking more than he claims. When the agreement on a specific activity is determined, often the momentum of the game is intensified to something not anticipated. This tactic is destructive because the male's intentions cannot be read, thus clandestinely giving double messages. As a result, it creates an atmosphere of

resentment and hostility rendered by the female. The lasting impression is that 'you can't trust a Black man no further than you can see him or throw him'. The female is left thinking that the male is only after one thing: sex! After this experience, the distrust is then perpetuated in future Black male/female relationships.

5) *Putting her to the test*
In pursuit of a secure relationship, the Black male will often 'put the female to the test'. It is the testing that often destroys the relationship. The male's general sentiment is that 'good girls do not engage in sex on the first date'. Therefore, the male will attempt to go beyond what is generally accepted in order to determine whether he is dating a 'good girl' or not. One of the motives of the game is designed to find a female that he feels he can trust. Often, men who distrust women play this game.

It has been said that the reason men play games is to hide the insecurities and vulnerabilities they feel. In fact, what men are really looking for is that special woman, who will love him unconditionally. However, the way these men are conditioned, they don't know how to go about achieving it, and once they get it, how to keep it. Unfortunately, the Black Vagina Finda isn't the only one caught up in this sordid lust affair. There is a female counterpart that is just as ruthless. Let's take a closer look.

The Low Pro Ho

While the male's primary purpose is sex, her agenda is two-fold. She has an unquenchable desire for 'penis and possessions'. This type of woman's identity is wrapped up in her sexuality and her ability to acquire material possessions. Most female players are similar to their male counterpart in that they believe they must control or conquer a man. So, they have taken on a macho stance toward relationships. There are many women who have serious issues with intimacy and fear intimacy and commitment with a man. Monogamy is seldom practiced. In fact, many women chose to only date.

Low Pro Hoes are equal opportunists. Because Black Vagina Findas have sexed women and gotten away with it for years, many feel as if it's time to return the favor. She will be just as ruthless as he to prove that she can win at the sex game. The problem is, many innocent bystanders are hurt and made victims in the process. Though it may shock you, many women desire sex just as much as men. They think about it, fantasize about it, crave it and will go to clubs, bars and social events to get it. I interviewed a woman who admitted that she would have sex two or three times a day with different men like clock work. Though she admitted that the sex wasn't that good, she continued to indulge because of her desire for physical gratification. Unfortunately, this woman is not alone and the numbers are growing at an alarming rate.

Shanice, 27, single
"I don't have low self-esteem. And I'm not in search for love. I just love sex. It feels good. I do what pleases me and I don't see anything wrong with that. I've never been in love and I don't feel I have to be in order to do something that makes my body feel good. Besides, if you get caught up in emotions, you set yourself up to get hurt. And frankly, I'd rather make someone a statistic than be one myself."

Tamika, 37, divorced twice
"I have had 29 sexual encounters in the course of one year. There were no strings attached. No feelings hurt. Even though I was never satisfied, I continued to have sex with men in order to seek vengeance on all the men who hurt me in my past. There was no touching, hugging or kissing. It was just straight sex. Once it was over, I would tell them all to leave."

Stacy, 23, single
"No man deserves me. I'm a good woman and I'm not impressed with what I see. I don't want a relationship because I'm selfish. All I accept are sponsors. Men who will take care of me. I get free meals, clothes, Chanel bags, and all of my financial needs taken

care of. Any man who wants a relationship must first start off as a sponsor before he can get to the next level with me. I'm not using them because I let them know in the beginning."

While a man's penis is often her delight, his ability to provide her with possessions creates another motivation in her mind. In an attempt to get what she wants, the Low Pro Ho has learned to use whatever is at her disposal. Since men crave sex the way a dog craves a bone, her body becomes her ultimate weapon. Therefore, her dress puts more emphasis on what she has to offer physically than intellectually. Often her outfit screams one bold and very clear message, "This can be yours if you come correct." Interestingly, many women will dress with half of their behind showing and nipples sticking through their blouses to attract a man. This is a woman who will give her body away in exchange for rent money, lavish vacations, or expensive gifts.

These Black women are driven to devise schemes to get gifts and money from men. Their attitudes toward men are simple: "Give me what I want, and I'll give you what you want." During a group discussion about women giving sex for money and possessions, one female defensively expressed, "I'd rather be a ho and get paid than a whore and get laid." With this attitude, she will look for any man who will give her more clothes, more presents, more gifts. If she can't find one, she may feel compelled to return to her former companion. In this kind of situation, it's "If you can't get what you want, take what you can get."

Low Pro Hoes will opt to be involved with a married or committed man because of a warped belief that they provide a greater sense of security than single men do. There are some Black women who will enter into a relationship and continue to relate to two or three spare men. After they get their side money and gifts from these men, plus the money and gifts from their main man, they've almost doubled their economic benefits.

The Low Pro Ho will succeed until men begin to see through her game. The following is a condensed list of games that they have mastered which is also found in David Burgest's article, *Sexual Games in Black Male/Female Relations.*

31

1) *I won't…If you don't or You can't…If you don't*
This game of sexual power is utilized by the Black female to control, manipulate and dominate the male. The notion is that the female sexuality is more valuable than the sexuality of the male. Therefore, the female is able to negotiate her body for favors in the relationship. She will, at times, withhold sexual involvement as a power play to gain other favors. Therefore, both the male and female view sex as a commodity on the stock exchange. This view has led to many broken relationships.

2) *I'm mad (angry) or I'll punish you*
This is a game played by the female in which sex is withheld as a form of punishment or revenge. In a marital relationship, sex is supposed to be a regular part of that union. Therefore, sex should be separated from disputes, arguments and disagreements. Withholding sex can become an expensive price to pay, resulting in damaged relationships.

3) *Looking for Mr. Right*
The premise of this game is that who you marry determines the success and outcome of a marriage rather than the ideas you both hold about marriage. When you seek to secure a mate who meets your innermost fantasies, it can easily become problematic. Fantasies can never be manifested into reality. Therefore, the hidden payoff can never be realized.

4) *What kind of girl do you think I am?*
This is a game played by the Black female early in the relationship. The intention of the game is to create a false sense of worthiness. The trick is to delude the male into thinking that she is a 'good girl' and that she would be a 'bad girl' if she entertained particular sexual or social proposals. A man attending a relationship seminar once said, "A man can't turn a ho into a house wife."

Because of the double standards that exist in our society, many women have become masters of deception. While men are applauded by society for their sexual explorations, women are often shunned. Therefore, many women chose not to be honest about their sexual history. So, once she engages in certain sexual activities, to deceive him, she will often respond with the one liner, "I've never done this before." This becomes problematic because eventually all the facades and false faces must come down. The male will eventually see her for who she really is and as a result, the game can possibly backfire and ultimately destroy the relationship.

5) *You can have me if you catch me; I love you*
This dangerous game can lead to an explosive reaction between two players. It's a perpetual game of 'catch me' and 'catch me again'. The Black female consciously flirts with members of the opposite sex while her mate looks on with jealousy. The purpose of the game is for the female to remain attractive to her present mate by demonstrating that other men are attracted to her.

Now that we've covered the games played by both men and women, let us look at the damaging effects of these games.

The Outcome

Every game must ultimately come to an end. It is at the conclusion of each game that a winner and loser are declared. In the world of sports, opponents show good sportsmanship by shaking each other's hands and going their separate ways. This behavior asserts the following message: "Good game and no hard feelings." Often when the game concept is placed within the confines of a male/female interpersonal relationship, there are hard feelings. A.L. Reynolds III, author of *Do Black Women Hate Black Men*, said it best when he wrote, "Until Black men and women confront the problem instead of each other, this deadly cycle of toxic relations will remain unbroken. Neither gender is more at fault than the other. There is equal fault and equal blame."

"Well, what is the problem?" you may ask. The Game. It is the sexual game where anything goes. It is the game where lies, deception, false pretenses, unrealistic expectations, and unrestrained sex are deployed. Games of this nature often create a win/lose or lose/lose outcome. The winner walks away in triumph, which in turn elevates their confidence and self-esteem. They will approach their next opponent with an overwhelming confidence of producing similar results. However, the loser's unexpressed feelings never die: they're buried alive and come forth later in uglier ways. Rage, cynicism and retaliation are often revealed. These emotions affect the quality of their self-esteem and eventually the quality of their relationships with others.

The responses of a hurt man and woman are distinctively different. When a man gets hurt it is much harder for him to become emotionally attached again. No matter how many women he may have, there will always be someone who will reject him. You (female reader) become the one he falls in love with. Every time he pursues a relationship with you, you adamantly deny him. Refusing to let go, he stalks you. He will camp outside your house, hidden in bushes. He will watch your every move. If you are seen with any other man, he will threaten to kill you. After filing the third restraining order against him, he will become bitter and develop animosity toward all women. He will turn into an ice cold and emotionally callous man who will continue to only relate to women sexually, if at all. He will lose all respect and trust for women. He will impregnate a woman and then abandon her. He'll dodge her calls and deny his own child. Well, what about women?

The old adage says, "Hell knows no fury like a woman scorned. " A Black Vagina Finda' can pull a certain nature out of a woman that he never knew existed. When a woman has been pushed to her limit—Watch Out! Pack your bags and head for the hills because if you don't, she'll get you. A scorned, vengeful, and mean spirited woman will key your car, slash your tires, and break every window. She will threaten your life, keep tabs on you and successfully sabotage your current relationship. She's angry and will hold you and every other man responsible. Is she crazy? Possibly. However, this type of outward frustration is generally a manifestation of her inner pain. She is hurt. And if you try to play a scorned woman's game by retaliating, you will lose every time.

When two hurt, very determined, stubborn, ego-invested individuals interact – the result is usually devastating. Blind to the fact that murder is also suicide because revenge is a two edged sword, many will become vindictive and want to get back or get even. This warlike philosophy creates adversarial conflict between both parties. Some people become so focused on an enemy, so totally obsessed with their behavior of another, that they become blind to everything except their desire for that person to lose, even if it means losing themselves. Then there is the person that is miserable and thinks that everyone else should be too. And the concept is simple. If no one is happy, perhaps being miserable isn't so bad.

The behavior of both men and women prove that there is a thin line between lust and hate. Sexual games and bedroom lies have become a perpetually destructive means of dealing with members of the opposite sex. The very thing that both men and women crave is that which keeps them furthest apart. So, to all of you reading this book who fall into the category of a Black Vagina Finda' or a Low Pro Ho, there is a better way. The vicious cycle of sex will ultimately destroy you. It will render you a spiritual death, a reprobate mind, and a depleted body. If this is you, there is still hope for a brighter future. You don't have to be the way that you are. My prayer is that, as you continue to read this book, your belief and behavior toward sex and relationships will change. So, to all you players, "Let the games end."

Black Thighs
Black Guys
&
Bedroom Lies

Chapter Two

MEETING IN MY BEDROOM

In today's society, premarital sex is far more widespread and accepted than it has been at any other point in our history. Men aggressively 'sow their oats' and female virgins are added to the endangered species list. A majority of Black singles now anticipate premarital sex. In fact, it is customary for two individuals to partake in a sexual exchange no later than their third meeting. For some, that may even be a stretch. According to a September 2000 *BET* poll, a whopping seventy-five percent of its viewers believe that sex on the first date is acceptable. Scary, don't you think?

Sex is no longer regarded as a sacred union between two covenant individuals. It has been reduced to a back seat or weekend-lodge experience with no emotional correspondence. Feelings are neither involved nor evoked by either party. Sex has merely become a physical indulgence for the sake of pleasure. Max

Elliot, author of *Ms. Thang: Real Knights Don't Show Up At Three in the Morning,* embraces and encourages this emotionless form of sex. Elliot, in her book, limits sex to nothing more than a physical experience. Elliot writes:

The human verifies this: sex evokes only the physiological, involuntary emotions of pain and pleasure. Immersing oneself in a tub of warm water can be pleasurable, or burning one's finger on a hot stove can be painful; both of these are also simply physiological responses...No it's not very romantic, but Queen Mothers understand that incorrectly linking physical attraction and emotion can sometimes be disastrous. So let's keep everything in perspective, okay? It helps to keep us from getting burned...Sex is a pumping, grinding, sweating, clinching, pinching, squeezing, teasing, shouting, vibrating, gliding, rocking, swaying, sucking, licking, fingering, peaking, falling, action between two or more human beings.

Elliot has erroneously limited the sexual experience to nothing more than a physical feeling. Many youth have embraced this same disturbing definition of sex. So, many youth precariously solicit sex for the sake of sex. Though there's much physical pleasure in the activity, many are left feeling physically and emotionally robbed.

Even in the midst of a relationship, if a partner is rewarded with sex too soon, the relationship can be short-circuited. If a partner's motivation for establishing a relationship is sexual curiosity, once that curiosity is satisfied, there is no longer any reason to stay. Touching, handling and fondling often distort the focus of a partner. Rather than focusing on the intimate affairs of a person's mind, emotions and spirit, all attention is transferred to the flesh. A desire to fondle each other's genitals supersedes a desire to discover each other's hidden qualities. These relationships are easily identifiable, because when two people are not wrapped up in the throes of passion, they have nothing to talk about.

This type of union can be classified as a sexship, not a relationship. A sexship is when the crux of the relationship is sexual in nature. Sex is the focus, the common interest and just about the only activity in which two individuals engage. Many people treat sex like food: something often used to satisfy the drive. It has been discussed in a very nonchalant way to describe what two people choose to do: "I'm going to go get me some" or "I know what's wrong with you, you need some."

The foundation of most of these sexual interactions is lust. Lust is nothing more than an intense desire or craving for something. It is an insatiable desire that can never be quenched. It is a feeling of intense, unrestrained sexual craving that seems to take one over. It's overwhelming and addictive. It will cause you to sleep with a stranger, cheat on a partner, commit a homosexual act, and put your whole life at risk. William McQueen, author of *The X-Rated Sex Book,* writes, "Except for money, sex is the only factor in our civilized societies that people contemplate at the risk of causing harm to themselves, their families, or to the loss of their jobs, and all for a few short hours of pleasure and a few seconds of orgasmic thrills...Sex, that obscure and yet paradoxically mundane, biological necessity, dominates us all in one way or another."

Too many suffer from an experience of powerlessness over a sexually compulsive behavior, resulting in unmanageable lifestyles. It's an addiction that causes shame, pain and self-loathing. The addict may wish to stop yet repeatedly fails to do so. Their uncontrollable desire for sex can be seen in the consequences they suffer: loss of relationships, difficulties with work, financial troubles, a loss of interest in things non-sexual, low self-esteem, and despair. There are many problems that can result from premarital sex.

The Bedroom: From Ecstasy to Expectancy

The bedroom has been transformed into a sexual marketplace and the bed has become the bartering table from which all transactions are made. It is comprised of three types of clientele: the sexual shopaholic, browser and bargain hunter who are busy negotiating deals. Sexual shopaholics are impulse shoppers that have sex based upon emotion and feeling. They'll embrace what is physically and visually appealing to the eye. All transactions are made out of pure want and desire, seldom need. Their addiction can never be quenched because they live a life of sexual consumption. Sexual browsers embrace the pleasure of others based upon limited information. They will often stumble across someone that stimulates their curiosity. After superficially familiarizing themselves with a prospect, sexual contact is made. Sexual bargain hunters generally make informed decisions. They'll spend considerable time getting to know someone before becoming sexually intimate. Once adequate information is provided and all doubt is gone, they'll jump headfirst into the throes of passion. However, the bedroom of sexual ecstasy often turns into the bedroom of expectancy.

What many choose to ignore is that once they enter into the bedroom, the stakes are high. Generally, when a man has sex with a woman, all he is concerned about is 'getting his'. Though that is the case with several women as well, women often have a lot more concerns before, during and after the act of sex. They suffer from sexual anxiety. "Will I contract a disease? What if I get pregnant? Will he stay? What will he think of me when it's all over? Will he lose respect for me? Is he here because he has a genuine interest or will he hit it and leave? All of these thoughts race through a woman's mind before, during and after sex. Unfortunately, many of her concerns manifest themselves. There are five things one can likely expect from the act of sex, not previously desired.

1) Emotional Anxiety

Many women find it difficult to distinguish the difference between sex and love. When they open their bedroom doors, they open their hearts as well. After earth-shattering sex, women often expect love in return. But a night of passionate sex seldom sparks the emotional intimacy frequently sought after. It rarely even motivates him to call back the next day. Typically, when an investment is made, it is normal to expect a return that exceeds the investment. However, when it comes to matters of the heart, many make investments that reap no return. Unfortunately, if a woman has sex before a relationship has had time to develop, she may feel attached to a stranger who may or may not feel a similar connection. Thus, creating a life of heartache and pain.

Though women attach themselves relatively quickly, men should not be counted out. According to Dr. Joyce Brothers in her book, *What Every Woman Should Know About Men* says, "A man usually succumbs to first-stage love long before his love object does. It has been established that men fall in love faster than women." Ironically, women may not express the same feelings for the men that fall head over heels for them. So, the love that they seek is not reciprocated. As a result of the emotional disparities that exist, many are left in pain.

2) Unrealistic Desire for Commitment

Sex will often lead to an unrealistic desire for commitment. It is often said that men will do anything for sex. They'll risk losing their jobs and families. Women, on the other hand, will do anything for a relationship. They'll sleep with a married man, support a deadbeat dad or suffer attacks from a verbally and/or physically abusive man. Women will even risk losing their family and friends if they are in love with a man. It's common for many women to offer their bodies to men in hopes of securing a level of commitment. These expectations are virtually never met.

When a woman gives herself away too easily, she loses worthiness in the eyes of men. Her body no longer holds its value. While it once was perceived as a precious jewel, it has become likened to a cheap piece of costume jewelry. Why, you may ask? It's simple. It is no longer a scarce commodity. A woman's most desired treasure has saturated the marketplace to such a degree that its worth has plummeted like a bad stock. It's the principle of supply and demand. If a man can easily sex a woman with no prior form of commitment, what will convince him to establish a commitment once the act is over? Generally nothing will. Most men won't buy the cow when the milk is free. So, it's not wise to use sex to try to keep a man. It is also not wise to have sex hoping love and commitment will follow.

3) Unplanned Pregnancy

Irresponsible sexual encounters can lead to unplanned pregnancy. Tiana was a graduating senior with hopes of a bright future. She was accepted to Georgetown University on a full academic scholarship. Tiana aspired to become a corporate attorney and own her own private practice. But her world came crashing down like a tidal wave. Three months before graduation Tiana discovered she was pregnant. She had been dating Terek for 3 ½ years and nothing had ever gone wrong. This can not be possible, she thought. She felt her law degree slip right through her fingers. A promising future was destroyed by one night of pleasure.

Sabrina was a twenty-six year old woman, pregnant with her eighth child. She didn't know the fathers of any of her children. Sex, for her, was a daily routine with no responsibility. Sabrina openly admitted to having with sex with well over 500 men. Several were married with children. Countless were one-night stands. Others were friends. In order to support her children, she prostituted, slept with several men for favors, and danced in strip clubs.

Whether your life parallels the experiences of Tiana or Sabrina, pregnancy is a life altering experience. It is an experience too familiar for many young Black females. According to the 2000 edition of the Baltimore Sun, single parents run almost 80 percent of all Black households. Most of these cases is the result of bearing children outside of wedlock. It is truly a scary statistic.

4) Disease

Irresponsible sexual encounters can also lead to disease. If there is any reason to stop having sex, it should be the possible threat of attracting a sexually transmitted disease. Despite all of the statistics, horror stories and personal experiences, sex is still an activity most would never consider stopping. The problem is that most people can't resist what they see and feel. So, in their minds they reason, if it feels good and looks good, it's all good. What they don't consider is that the sexiest pair of legs can be infested with Herpes. The most luscious lips can be dripping with Gonorrhea. Numerous people have been guilty of putting their mouths and body parts in places that they have no knowledge of. Many even get rid of condoms because they think their partners have no STD.

This behavior has led many down the path of no return. Black people are 30 times more likely to be infected with a sexually transmitted disease than their white counterpart. According to a special report done by *Ebony Magazine*, AIDS is the Number 1 killer of Black people under the age of 55. Even though Blacks are only 12 percent of the population, they account for 45 percent of all reported AIDS cases in the United States. Black females account for a whopping 60 percent of American women with the disease. Beyond that, women have been left infertile due to internal bodily damage from sexually transmitted diseases. Some women have even undergone biopsies for pre-cancerous conditions due to having too many sexual partners. To top it all off, the CDC reports nearly 100 new cases of AIDS among Blacks every day.

5) Death

Sexual encounters often lead to death, particularly among Black youth. According to the Children's Defense Fund, every 20 hours a Black child or Black young adult under the age of 23 dies from causes related to HIV. Many of the incurable diseases that people attract during sex often lead to death. Proverbs 5:11-13 says: *"And you groan and mourn when your end comes, when your flesh and body are consumed, And you say, How I hated instruction and discipline, and my heart despised reproof! I have not obeyed the voice of my teachers nor submitted and consented to those who instructed me (AMP)."* Another translation simply says, *"Afterward you will groan in anguish when disease consumes your body" (NLT).* While many lie on the deathbed of sexual sin, they die a slow death of regret. They reflect on every warning and instruction they'd ever received. They reflect on every sexual act performed that has put them in their predicament.

Sex is not worth dying for. No man or woman is that fine. No one is that irresistible. Even though people are aware of the dangers of sex, they engage in it as if there are no ramifications. Such behavior is extremely suicidal. It is like playing Russian

Roulette. You are giving someone else the authority to take your life from you. Every one you have sex with outside of marriage should be regarded as a potential murderer. All it takes is one microscopic germ to get inside of your body, multiplying itself until it ultimately consumes you. This drawn-out process leads to one thing: termination.

Secrets, Lies & Deception

Shhhh, there are certain sexual secrets that you should never tell. Right? Well, all sexual secrets are different. Someone with an extensive sexual history might be concerned, for example, about appearing to be too experienced. Some people choose to hide personal feelings and desires. Many disguise their behavior and remain secretive about their sexual past.

However, where secrets dwell, deception is conceived and lies are birthed. Relationships are comprised of people who wear masks and hide behind false faces. Initial interactions start with lengthy phone calls, romantic gestures, special dates and lots of time spent getting to know each other. After feeling totally comfortable with someone and ready to offer your heart, "Wham!," a bone falls out of the closet of your partner's past. Comfort is lost. Tension arises. While the crushing revelation rolls off the tongue of the confessor, an intense feeling of disgust and betrayal begins to sift through the recipient's mind. Their heart starts to palpitate. Their eyes begin to squint with rage as silent tears roll down their face. A nauseous sensation consumes every crevice of their body. A loud, deafening silence fills the air.

How did this all start? It started with one secret shamefully covered up by just one word: a lying word, a word full of deception. It all started with one word that temporarily hid the iniquities of the past. Perhaps it was a secret of homosexual indulgence, a rapist predisposition, excessive promiscuity, or incestuous activity. Whatever they may be, untold secrets can destroy relationships.

Most men and women usually lie about their amount of sexual partners, their frequency of sexual encounters and their vast knowledge of sexual thrills. Women generally lie because they feel that if they act as if they know too much about sex, they will appear trampy. Men generally lie because they feel that most women can't handle the truth. Men, generally, feel uncomfortable if their partner is more sexually experienced than they are. Likewise, many women feel insignificant once they discover the amount of women their partner has experienced. As a result of these insecurities, most opt to keep the secret or live a lie.

Some things are better left unsaid. However, in a very sure relationship each mate should feel secure enough to discuss any issue of a confidential nature with respect and tact. If the secret is relevant to the present relationship, the truth must be told. Most people don't tell really intense secrets until they reach a point where they feel safe and secure in the relationship. And it's hardly ever in the beginning. But, the sooner the matters are discussed, the better. It is better to speak the truth than to live with the fear, deceit, and shame that comes from hiding the truth from your mate. Unless you are honest about past sexual sin, you won't be able to understand the potential challenges you'll confront because of it. Though confessing may risk the security of the bond, in the end the relationship will be much stronger if you are dealing with a fairly balanced person.

Masturbation: A Dead-End Street

Sexual behavioral study and research prove it has been conservatively estimated that the average American male ejaculates 5,000 times in his lifetime. That is roughly equal to 4 gallons of fluid. A single ejaculation has 200 to 500 million sperm cells. So, there is enough sperm lost in one spilling to populate the entire United States. Multiplying this figure by 5,000 ejaculations per lifetime, a man has the capacity to provide seed for approximately 2.5 trillion human lives. Within a man's loins sits the capacity to produce more than two hundred times the present

45

population of the four billion people on the planet earth. So, a male's sexual energy, if stockpiled, is literally more potent than an atomic bomb. Just as an atomic bomb is used to erupt and cause an explosion within the earth, many men look for a fertile dwelling place (vagina) to erupt into. Whether or not they can sexually erupt in a woman's vagina, they'll often establish a personal relationship with themselves (masturbation).

Masturbation has always been a dirty little secret hidden behind the veils of individuals' private lives. Ironically, people would rather confess a promiscuous lifestyle than a habitual act of self-indulgence. For years, masturbation has been noted solely as a male activity. However, with a shift in societal norms, more and more women are admitting to the once detestable act of masturbation. National polls, surveys and statistics report that men and women are neck in neck with their acceptance and practice of the activity.

Masturbation has become a sexually addictive activity. Clara, a 21-year-old student at Greensboro College, admitted to masturbating three to four times a week. That's just about every other day. Her self-stimulation frequently involved the use of a dildo she kept in the drawer of her night table. She often masturbated before dates to overcome sexual anxiety and at the end of hectic days to release tension. Twenty-three-year-old William, on the other hand, suffered from a more severe problem. Masturbation consumed his life. 'Girly' magazines, porn flicks, pictures of past and present girlfriends, jars of Vaseline, and a vast imagination were the tools William used to fulfill his lustful desires. There was no method to his madness. There were times when William masturbated six times a day. He often felt the urge to masturbate at the most awkward times. He would masturbate in restaurants, classrooms, movie theatres, public bathrooms, and even while driving.

Whether you casually masturbate or suffer from an addiction, the results can be potentially devastating. Many physicians have argued that masturbation is a normal and healthy act of self-indulgence. Their position is often attributed to the wonders of self-discovery. Unfortunately, the societal acceptance of masturbation has led to increasingly alarming youthful activity.

According to a *Details* Magazine Book College Sex Survey, eighty-six percent of men and seventy-four percent of women believe that masturbation is not only healthy, but also necessary. However, findings of the effect that masturbation has on the human body aren't favorable.

Ejaculation of the male sperm for purposes other than procreation is considered a wasteful loss of extremely precious fluid. Some scholars have considered one drop of semen equal in vital power to one hundred drops of blood. Blood in the body is used to sustain life. So, imagine how much more important semen must be. Mantak Chia, author of *Taoist Secrets of Love: Cultivating Male Sexual Energy,* explains the consequences of losing semen.

"With frequent ejaculation of sperm, vitality ultimately plummets. The big spender loses stamina, his vision begins to weaken, hair tumbles from the skull: he grows old before his time. At first he will not feel drained, but after years of abuse his capacities will begin to drop alarmingly. When the hormonal secretions of the sexual glands are regularly leaked out, the body is sapped of its root. Within a period of time that will range from months to decades depending on the endowment of the individual, creative and sexual abilities are halved, and the ability to withstand disease and frailties of old age is diminished...The organs of digestion will be unable to assimilate sufficient nutritional energies to replace those irrecoverable life energies lost by ejaculations. When men abuse the reproductive function, the secretions of the sexual glands are lost...resulting in mental and physical weakness, inability to concentrate, and a less tenacious memory."

Similarly, doctors have shared that women secrete fluids every time orgasm is reached. The depletion of women's vaginal secretions result in the depletion of nutrients the body needs to properly function. Though there are more alarming concerns with men, women are not exempt. So, after knowing the damaging affects it has on the body, it would be foolish to continually engage in such activity. Proverbs 26:11 says, *"As a dog returns to his vomit, so a fool repeats his folly (TLB)."* Such is the same when a man or woman masturbates.

Not only is masturbation detrimental to your body, but to your spirit alike. Masturbating actually feeds the flesh's appetite. The more the appetite is fed, the more it grows. Meanwhile, the spirit is starved of its spiritual nutrients, the word of God. It is the word of God that instructs you on how to conduct your body. 1 Thessalonians 4:3-5 says: *"For this is the will of God, that you should be consecrated (separated and set apart for pure and holy living): that you should abstain and shrink from all sexual vice (sin), That each one of you should know how to possess (control, manage) his own body in consecration (purity, separated from things profane) and honor, Not [to be used] in the passion of lust like the heathen, who are ignorant of the true God and have no knowledge of His will (TLB)."* Now that you know what the Word says concerning the purpose and function of your body, walk in the Spirit and live sexually pure.

No matter how creatively one masturbates, masterbation remains a temporary fix that cannot satisfy. It's a short-lived experience that keeps one coming back for more. It's a desire that can never be quenched. However, it is more than just a physical longing. It is more of an appetite of the mind. The mind is the place where the imagination resides. It is also the largest sexual organ in the body. The act of masturbation forces the mind to relive past sexual experiences or envision future fantasies. It is the mental stimulation that brings an individual to ejaculation. Therefore, when you masturbate you become a slave to your carnal (sensual) mind. The Bible declares that carnality leads to spiritual death because a lustful mind is complete hatred towards God. The biblical solution to controlling the mind is found in 2 Corinthians 10:5. *"Casting down imaginations, and every high thing that exalteth (elevates) itself against the knowledge of God, and bringing into capacity every thought to the obedience of Christ (KJV)."* If the Bible says to think on pure things and you're imagining what sex would be like with someone, that thought has to be brought into captivity. All lustful thoughts that are contrary to the word of God must be quickly destroyed. So, in order to truly conquer and destroy the spirit of masturbation, you must simply starve your flesh and feed your spirit.

Just Friends

Black people represent the ethnic group with the largest number of singles in America. Many either choose not to marry or if they do, wind up in divorce court soon thereafter. Even among singles, relationships have lost their worthiness. Lust is more familiar than love in this society. Media outlets such as movies, television, and magazines virtually provide road maps to lust. Lust can never commit to anyone or anything because the lustful feeling can disappear as quickly as it arrives. Love, on the other hand, is seen more as a risk or a mystery. There are no identifiable road maps that lead to love. For many, it represents the most feared uncharted territory in the world. Therefore, people have given up on relationships for many different reasons. Generally, men run from relationships because they fear commitment. Settling down with one woman is a scary phenomenon for many men. Women, on the other hand, offer a multitude of reasons for giving up on relationships.

Many women who can't establish a committed relationship are guilty of settling for the next best thing: a sexship. Men draw them into a sexship instead of a well-balanced, committed relationship. They offer sex in hopes of eventually winning a man into a relationship. However, it is often not until their heart is broken that many women learn that giving sex to a man may give them certain things, but commitment is usually not one of them. Very few sexships turn into long-term, committed, quality relationships. Sexships come and go, but Women hold onto these sexships for a sense of fulfillment and companionship that does not last.

Many career-oriented women choose to remain single. Relationships are viewed as very time consuming, thus requiring too much attention and care. With a focus on financial and occupational pursuits, relationships aren't a priority. Consumed with late-night meetings, frequent business trips and never-ending paperwork, relationships are deemed unrealistic. Therefore, many women befriend men whom they interact with on a need-to-sex-basis.

For other women, after being hurt and disappointed in countless relationship, they become tired. So, rather than deal with the strain of relationships, many opt to have sexual dealings with no relational strings attached. They will treat themselves to sex because it feels good. Rather than constantly becoming vulnerable, many choose to sex men until they find their soul mate. This way, in her mind, nobody gets hurt. They claim they can handle uncommitted sex for sex's sake. Women often advise their 'sistah-girls' to keep a man on the side for sexual emergencies until Mr. Right comes along. Many believe they can have sex and not care about the man. Besides, using someone to fulfill your physical desires with no strings attached is easier than dealing with the overwhelming responsibility of maintaining a relationship. For this reason women settle for 'booty calls' and one-night stands.

Max Elliot, author of *Ms. Thang: Real Knights Don't Show Up At Three in the Morning*, encourages such careless sexual behavior which contradicts the title of her book. In her book, she writes "Sometimes single Sistah-Girls, whatever their age, just want to get some. We simply want to have sex – no romance, no lovemaking, and no mating ritual – just sex. We wake up in the middle of the night or, like me, can't go to sleep and don't feel like masturbating. So, we reach for the telephone and make the call...Mama always said if you got an itch, scratch it. So, like I said, my sisters, go ahead, make the call."

Both men and women have taken on this irresponsible activity. Late-night or early-morning calls lead to nothing more than a lustful exchange between two consenting individuals. Though there are no emotions required to partake in such an activity, there is usually a connection between the caller and the callee. The connection represents a certain level of trust and familiarity the two parties have with each other. Though each person is free to sex whomever they choose, the connection between the two helps them justify their activity as being more than meaningless casual sex. But, as soon as the deed is done, they part and go their separate ways. There is no pillow talk, no waking up in each other's arms, no hope for a future. It is a cheap thrill that never satisfies. Rather than filling a void, such casual sex creates emptiness and a need that can never be met.

Though the so called 'friend' or sex buddy may seem convenient, they offer no long-term fulfillment and leave all parties involved emotionally and spiritually bankrupt.

Lonely Ladies

Many women equate success with finding a good man, getting married and raising a family. Young or old, women feel as if they are not complete unless they have a man. Women love the feeling of being loved, cherished and taken care of. But when a woman becomes desperate for companionship, she is destructive to herself and to other parties involved.

Few people embrace their season of singleness as a time to focus on and celebrate the joys and accomplishments of self. Rather, the state of being alone causes several to fall into the deplorable pit of loneliness. Loneliness is a condition that doesn't discriminate. Neither does desperation. The undesirable state of loneliness often leads to desperation. Desperate women can be beautiful or unattractive, working or unemployed, and college graduates or high school dropouts. It really doesn't matter.

This is a woman who will stop at nothing to get what she wants. She will wear provocative attire that exposes her breasts, butt, thighs, and legs. She will date no good men and even refuse to leave physically and mentally abusive relationships for companionship's sake. Why? The thought of being alone is frightening. This fear will cause a desperate woman to aggressively pursue, wrongfully date and shamelessly sex any man who turns her on. It doesn't matter if he's married, engaged, shacking, or seriously involved. In fact, some women intentionally seek out men who are in relationships because man-sharing has become desirable. She will justify her actions by thinking that the man is the other woman's responsibility, not hers. She will often convince herself that she is somehow what that man needs. This is a woman who is cold-hearted and careless.

A desperate woman will often give her body away to anyone who asks. Why? She feels it is the only way to get and keep a man. But if you use your body to bring a man into a relationship that is what you'll have to continue to use to maintain that relationship. No matter how much a man may want a woman, anytime she gives herself away too easily, she will lose worthiness in the eyes of that man. Besides, how can any man value a woman who doesn't value herself? This type of woman is easily identifiable and men will often take advantage of a woman's vulnerable state.

A lonely woman makes finding a man a relentless mission. In pursuit of her narrow-minded goal, she quickly becomes a relational rebel without a pause. She will create an alluring and irresistible niche that will intentionally separate her from the rest of other women in order to give her a competitive edge in the pursuit of snaring a man. Some women will attempt to get to a man's heart by perfecting their culinary skills and regularly cooking to a man's personal delight. Others will seek to cultivate sexual talents by reading sex magazines, watching porno movies and consulting other men. Many are known to obsessively diet and workout in an effort to sculpt a perfect body that can make any man drop to his knees. Several women have even resorted to letting a man live in her home rent-free, buying him expensive gifts, baby-sitting his children and continually lending him money amongst many other things. Depending on the level of desperation, some women will even deceive a man into thinking that she's on birth control and intentionally get pregnant in order to trap a man into a relationship. What they don't understand is that if a man doesn't want to commit to them, he certainly won't commit to their baby. If he does, it will further destroy any hopes of a fulfilling relationship.

Loneliness is one of the major reasons women seek companionship. Women often fall into one-night stands out of their need to be loved by someone. In their pursuit to find intimacy, all they wind up with is sexuality. Bishop T.D. Jakes once said, "Sexuality without intimacy feels like rape." Many women have been raped mentally, physically or spiritually. This unhealthy need for affirmation and validation has caused many women to travel down a self-destructive path of promiscuity, addiction, self-neglect, and overall unhappiness. But, wholeness can never be met by turning to the arms of another person. It can only come from establishing a relationship with God. Only God can restore the love, joy and fulfillment that are often sought in other men. But, if your focus is wrong, it will lead to more hurt and disappointment.

Shacking Up

Couples often offer a variety of reasons as to why they choose to live together before marriage. Many respond that cohabitation is economically feasible. Rather than have a couple pay two separate rents or mortgages, it financially makes more sense to have one expense and save for the future. Ironically, these financial goals are rarely met. Some conform to this living arrangement due to convenience. Many couples often travel across town and spend several nights a week at each other's apartment. They believe that they're living together anyway, just in two different locations. Therefore, it makes more sense to select one place of residence. The birth of a child is often a reason couples decide to move in as well. The thought often becomes, "If we are willing to start a family, we might as well live like one." Though there are countless reasons people offer to justify their living arrangements, most couples decide to move-in together with plans of marriage. However, most couples end up with no sign of wedding bells. In fact, the average length of time most cohabiting couples remain in marriages is about one year.

Cohabitation has become commonplace over the last few decades. As a matter of fact, more than half of all marriages are preceded by cohabitation. According to the Census Bureau Report, unmarried couples living together in 1998 topped 4,236,000, up from 439,000 in 1960. However, such arrangements were only designed for married couples. In fact, there was a time when couples living together outside the confines of marriage were considered to be 'living in sin.'

Living together was designed as an activity exclusively for individuals within the season of marriage. Well, are there consequences for participating in such a lifestyle outside of ones appointed season? Certainly! Operating out of ones season will assure a life that will ultimately function out of order. When someone's life is out of order, destruction soon follows. Not only can it destroy the partner, but it has the potential to destroy the relationship as well.

It has been proven that people who 'shack up' break up. This lifestyle often leads to delays in marriage, increases in divorce, increased risk of domestic violence for women and the risk of physical and sexual abuse to children. According to *The National Survey on Families and Households* of the University of Wisconsin, marriages that are preceded by living together have 50 percent higher disruption (divorce or separation) rates than marriages without premarital cohabitation. In fact, of 100 couples who cohabit, 40 couples will break up before the marriage, and 45 will divorce or separate. That leaves only 15 lasting marriages out of 100 trial marriages or cohabiting experiences. While there is more sex between unmarried cohabitants than between married couples (one more act per month), there's also more cheating by both partners. Each year a couple lives together, the more likely they are to become unfaithful. Couples who cohabit are 40% more likely to cheat than those couples who don't. One woman, after separating from her former lover stated, "I believe I was violated, abused and used because I was a sexual playmate for months. And then when he got ready to marry, he married someone else."

Dr. Ron Elmore, author of *How To Love A Black Woman*, says, " Cohabitation is a substitute for permanent commitment and intimacy. It's an appealing one. It's a seductive one. It's a fun one. It saves money. It does a bunch of good things. But the one good thing that we're really looking for is one person who is willing to say 'Til death do us part', I love you, and I plan to be here with you until good, until bad, no matter what. And that is not a part of the contract of living together. It's not required. And when we don't require those things of ourselves, we don't get those things from others."

The issue of permanent commitment (marriage) is seldom talked about in any serious way. The longer two individuals live together, the more unrealistic marriage becomes. So, if you're considering 'shacking up' before saying 'I do', understand that that day may never come. Though your desire for marriage may be genuine, your partner's desire may differ. Let's just keep it real. Your partner's probably thinking, "Why buy the milk if I've already got some heifer (cow) laying up in my bed?" Think about it. If you've benefited from watching free cable for months without paying, would you request your cable provider to bill you? Of course not, it's free. The same principle applies to marriage. "Why get married to live a lifestyle that I'm already living?" Though living together may seem like a wonderful idea, it will most likely ruin any chance you may have for a brighter future.

Choose Abstinence

Abstinence in a relationship helps cultivate genuine intimacy. Besides, sex is much more than a physical exercise. Sex is actually a covenant sign that marks the sanctity and sacredness of a marriage. Sex normally represents a bonding between two people. If a person has sex with someone before a relationship is established either party can find themselves emotionally connected to a stranger who may not feel the same way.

Premarital sex isn't wrong simply because two ready bodies come together. Something more meaningful is happening. When two separate entities come together they create a new thing. Sodium and chloride produce salt. Two hydrogen molecules and one oxygen molecule produce water. Likewise, when you engage in physical intimacy with another person, the engagement creates a new thing: the two people become one. Now, at any time should you decide that you no longer want the new thing that has been created, if it was just a simple act of sex, you must pull away. However, in that pulling away, you tear away a part of yourself.

Tony Evans, author of *Sexual Purity,* declares: "The more times you engage in this destructive process, the more of you is left behind and the greater the damage. Anyone who has kids knows what it's like trying to get chewing gum out of the carpet, especially after someone has stepped in it. It's a traumatic experience trying to pull that gum without leaving any behind. Something almost mystical has happened. The merger of the gum with the fiber in the carpet has so integrated them that to get out all the gum, you have to tear away some of the carpet too. And you usually leave some of the gum behind anyway. You may get a lot of it out, but there is always that residue. So it is when there is a merger of two people in sexual intercourse. When they try to tear that relationship apart, they tear themselves, and a part of them is left behind." Therefore, sexual union was not designed to initiate a relationship, but to *consummate* a permanently committed marriage relationship.

Black Thighs
Black Guys
&
Bedroom Lies

The Game

Meeting In My Bedroom

School Days

Somebody's Sleeping In My Bed

Whatever Happened to Black Love?

Don't Wanna Be A Playa No More

Good Lovin'

Chapter Three

SCHOOL DAYS

From New Orleans to Nashville, New York City, Chicago, Houston, Charlotte, St. Louis, Baltimore and Atlanta, the *Black Thighs, Black Guys & Bedroom Lies College Tour* was now underway. Mesmerizing thousands of college students all over this nation at national conventions, regional conferences and college and university campuses was a gratifying experience.

However, the most intense experiences have always been on college and university campus. Why? It's simple. The culture of a college campus is like no other. By day it is an academic and socially oriented environment. It is a place where students attend large lecture halls, study group sessions, and an occasional student organization meeting. Computer labs are full of students typing homework assignments and term papers. Student centers are constantly invaded by credit card companies offering free t-shirts, hats and mugs for anyone who will sign up for a card. Cafeterias are saturated with different food smells and polluted with the sounds of forks dropping, plates banging and stomachs growling. Fraternity and sorority members are dressed in an array of bright colors as they compete in step shows on the yard. The whole campus is governed by the periodic chime of the bell tower perfectly positioned in the center court of the campus. These are some of the daily customs that students experience by day.

But in the midnight hour, when the sun has gone down and all of the lights have gone out, the typical college campus is transformed from an institution of higher learning to an underworld of erotic lust and sexual showdowns. Dormitories are transformed into learning institutions and testing facilities. And, though students declare various majors, lust and self-gratification are the core curriculum. Many engross themselves in sex parties, freak shows, orgies, and *menage a trios*. They randomly grab breasts, penises and vaginas, not even knowing whom they belong to.

Students are often caught climbing up and down dorm building fire escapes in the middle of the night, having sex with their midnight lovers while roommates are present. Sorority members have at times performed sexual favors for their brother fraternity members. Fraternity houses, also known as sexual slaughterhouses, provide living space for Greek-lettered men to sex women while being videotaped, photographed or merely observed through peepholes and windows. Female students even sleep with their professors for passing grades. As a result of all this sexual activity, many students graduate early with their P.H.D., their *Pimp and Hoes Degree*.

Dormitories across the nation are houses haunted by legions of sexual spirits creeping throughout corridors, stairwells and sleeping quarters. Upon entering these buildings, I have often inhaled the foul stench of sordid sex, ineffectively disguised by incense. I have faintly heard the moans and groans of pleasure exchanged between two willing and consenting hard bodies. But, I have also heard the faint cries for help by women being raped, whose voices were drowned out by loud, deafening music. I could see the body-like shadows of methodical shifting performed behind curtained windows. I have even heard men masturbating in bathroom stalls, releasing their life force. While dormitories have become a fantasyland for most, they have also become sex dungeons of no escape.

Unfortunately, on college campuses there is a tremendous pressure to loose one's virginity. College is the one place on earth that offers young people the chance to finally be free. Campus life gives students the opportunity to act out all of their suppressed and hidden sexual desires. It is the first chance to explore their sexuality openly, to experiment freely without the burdens of parents, curfews, and easily assigned labels. So, lots of formerly sheltered youth, who haven't seen, heard or experienced much in life, rush off to school and go 'buck wild'.

Universities across the country offer 'porn studies' in their course load, though these are often hidden under titles like 'community studies.' These institutions have courses that require students to produce pornography for their final exam. Professors instruct their students that nothing would be considered too risqué on the final exam. Universities even sponsor pornography conferences on campus grounds. Exposure to such behavior allows many students to adopt a very liberal approach toward sex.

As a result, students regard sex as an extra-curricular activity--nothing more, nothing less. Many have lied, tricked and deceived others in order to sexually take advantage of them. They live in a world where everyone keeps track of who and how many they've slept with. Freshmen aren't considered anything but pieces of fresh meat. It's nothing but a game. It's a game of one-night stands. It's a game where people sit in college cafeterias hawking both men and women, seeking their next sex partner. It's a game in which people strive to become campus legends.

The Campus Legend

Tina was a first-year student at a mid-sized university in the hills of Allentown, Pennsylvania. So striking and stunning was her appearance, she often received the stares of both men and woman. This fair-skinned beauty would strut around in a voluptuous frame often accented with provocative attire. Tight and revealing was the code she bore. Exuding such an erotic aura, Tina welcomed the sexual proposals of many men. Without hesitation, she shamelessly slept with a fellow incoming freshman midway into the school's first day.

"I don't think I was as sexually active as my friends who were sleeping with their boyfriends in high school; I waited until I left home and went away to school. And once I got a taste of college life I hated waking up alone, hated going to bed alone, hated always thinking about sex, and hated never having any. My body was adjusted to making love on a regular basis, and it has now become more of an overwhelming desire, certain to receive regular fulfillment." Tina's insecurities clouded her sexual judgment with men and her insatiable desire for sex prompted her to entertain an excessive amount of men night after night.

Merely six weeks into the semester, Tina successfully slept with 35 different men. She was very open about her sexuality and didn't care who knew. To affirm her newfound sexual freedom, she placed a very detailed list of her sex partners on the outside of her dorm room door. The list consisted of football and basketball players, fraternity members, and non-Greek men, resident directors and even geeks for whom she felt sorry.

Tina's adventurous sexual pursuits drove her to have sex in cars, parks, locker rooms, rooftops, empty classrooms, school parking lots, tennis courts, swimming pools, on pool tables and in window sills. Ironically, she let men put their penis between her legs but wouldn't allow them to put their tongue in her mouth. "Kissing represents intimacy and I'm not trying to get intimate. That's not what I'm in this for. I love the thrill of sex and I just want to be sexually fulfilled," she explained.

While some felt what Tina was doing was detestable and degrading to women, many were intrigued by her brash behavior. While men eagerly waited to be placed on her list, Tina persuaded her friend and sexual thrill-seeking equal, Nikki, to join in on her sex sessions. This newly established sexual tag team had soon become the talk of the campus. Tappan Hall, room 304 had now become a sexual playground for all interested prospects. There was no restraint placed on who and how many could join. While entertaining company, Tina and Nikki often played very loud music to overshadow the screaming, panting, squeaking of bed mattresses, and banging of headboards against dorm room walls. With the help of Nikki, the list soared to 50. The new names consisted of both men and women. They often slept with other women's men, as well as other men's women. Placed next to each name were triangles, circles and squares signifying what sort of sexual activities were performed. Triangles represented a threesome, circles represented an orgy and squares represented a foursome. Numerous symbols by any one person's name indicated a person's repetitious involvement.

By the end of the semester, both Tina and Nikki had become campus legends. However, what was once admired by many, soon became despised by most. Within a semester, they went from first to worse. They faced insurmountable ridicule and criticism. They were labeled 'Easy Skeezees'. What was once Tappan Hall Dormitory soon became 'The Hall of Scanks'. Unfortunately, their reputation followed them wherever they went. Men would no longer look at or touch them. Every sorority on campus pledged to bar both women from sisterhood for life. And signs with 'slut,' 'bitch' and 'whore' were often plastered on their dorm-room doors. Overcome with guilt and embarrassment, for the remaining four years, Tina and Nikki never left their rooms.

Although men have generally filled the shoes of campus legends, this story is all too familiar for many women on college campuses. According to the *Details Magazine Book College Sex Survey*, 86% of women are sexually active compared to the 74% of sexually active men. While men have admitted to having more sexual partners than their female counterparts, women have admitted to having more sexual encounters. Forty-eight percent of women have sex more than once a week compared to the thirty-five percent of men. Similarly, thirty-one percent of women have sex two or three times a week compared to the twenty-five percent of men. In addition, twenty-eight percent of women, more than double the thirteen percent of men, think about sex once a day. So, never let it be said that certain women aren't as sexually obsessed as men. The college experience is one of the rare cases in which women exceed men in sexual behavior.

Unprotected Sex

What is most alarming about the sexual activity of students on college campuses is that unprotected sex runs rampant. Sex on campus has become an activity that 'just happens' and many students have taken on the hellish idea 'If it feels good, do it'. A campus survey reported that 47% of students had engaged in sexual intercourse when they had not planned to, but did it as a result of alcohol, peer pressure, availability, or desire. This phenomenon has created an atmosphere of unprotected sex. In his article "Sexuality on Campus," Toby Simon explains:

"It is easy to understand how anyone gets carried away in the throes of passion. The intensity of the moment can make it difficult for people to stop doing what they are doing to talk about protection and find a condom...Sex feels good, and the part of the body that feels the best has no brain. As a result, unprotected intercourse takes place, and a variety of outcomes follow. It is often after one such passionate unprotected love making session that students decide to be more cautious next time."

Unfortunately, 'next time' becomes a repeat performance of the last time. The more unprotected sex is practiced, the more it is justified. When asked why men refused to wear condoms, the reasons varied:

1. I can't feel it if I use a condom.
2. It's not really sex if a condom is involved.
3. I can please a woman better without a condom.
4. I can't climax by using a condom.
5. I don't want to spoil the mood by stopping to get a condom.
6. I'm drunk or high and forget about wearing a condom.
7. I've convinced my partner that I don't have anything and don't need a condom.
8. It was a spur-of-the-moment decision and I didn't have a condom.
9. I simply don't care.

This twisted and very dangerous view that men have about sex has left many women pregnant or victims of unwanted sexually transmitted diseases. Having sex without a condom is like going bungee jumping without the cord; it's just plain stupid. Because of such behavior, college students are now ranking higher than the national average for the risk of HIV infection. Robert Redfield Jr., an AIDS research professional, boldly stated that the next wave of increased HIV infections will be among African-American college students.

In a study of risk behavior among students, it was concluded that the "sensation seeking predisposition" of college students combined with a "sexual motive for a pleasurable relationship" has a direct effect upon all areas of sexual behavior, including number of partners and incidents of unprotected sex. Interestingly, this sexual behavior is not birthed on college campuses--it's just reinforced their. Many students have brought this behavior in from their former high schools. Everyday it is estimated that over 15,000 high school students in America are infected with at least one sexually transmitted disease. Everyday, 33,000 people get a new STD and 22,000 of them are between the ages of 15 and 24 years old.

Anal and oral sex are the riskiest forms of sex, as they relate to the transmission of HIV. Sixty-eight percent of men and seventy-two percent of women admitted to never using a condom during anal sex. Since the anus is smaller and less flexible than the vagina, tears can occur in the tissue in and around the anus, even if you are very careful. These tears make it very easy to transmit or contract a blood-borne disease such as HIV and/or AIDS. Seventy-seven percent said they never use a condom or dental dam during oral sex. Any nick or abrasion on your gums or tongue could be an opening for AIDS. So, whether giving or receiving oral sex, there is a strong possibility of being infected.

Sadly, of these students who were reported on, more women report contracting sexually transmitted diseases than men for one simple reason: it's easier for a man to infect a woman than for a woman to infect a man. A man with any kind of STD, including HIV, may infect six out of ten women he has intercourse with, while a woman with the same disease would probably infect one or two of her ten partners.

Condoms (How Safe Are They)

So the answer is condoms, right? Wrong! Dr. Edwin Louis Cole relied on scientific research data when he wrote, "Condoms cannot stop sexually transmitted diseases that spread from outside contact such as syphilis, herpes, and crabs, to name a few. The HIV virus itself is 450 times smaller than a sperm cell, about one-fifth the size of the holes in latex – the material from which the best condoms are made. So, these super small viruses can get through a hole in a condom much more easily than sperm can. The transmission of HIV can be compared to a ping-pong ball going through a basketball hoop. It's just that easy."

For example, the HIV virus is so small that two million of the disease causing agents could crowd on the period at the end of a sentence. The average failure rate for preventing the transmission of HIV was 31 percent. Condoms provide considerably less protection against sexually transmitted diseases than they do against pregnancy.

Condoms also fail up to 36% of the time against pregnancies for those depending on them the most: young people. That means that one out of every three teenage couples using condoms will become pregnant each year.

Deep, isn't it? But that's not all. Condoms have expiration dates on them. Just as milk, cheese, bread, and other food products spoil, so do condoms. University of Pennsylvania, Dr. Loretta Sweet Jemmott, sites an experiment in which students sent to buy condoms in a predominantly Black neighborhood discovered that many of the condoms had already expired. An expired condom won't protect you from anything. Ironically, manufacturing defects of condoms seem to always wind up in the Black community. One would think that Kellogg's manufactured condoms sent to these Black districts because they have an overwhelming tendency to snap, crackle and pop. According to the Seventeenth Revised

Edition of the textbook *Contraceptive Technology*, "27,000 condoms slip or break on the average night."

The problem is that twisted linguistics and perverted facts of most sex educators have misled youth. Flowery phrases like "safe sex" and "responsible behavior" offer promises of pleasure with "protection". For instance, the West Allis' *Curriculum Guide* claims that condoms are 90-97% effective and the leading cause of condom failure is the misuse of condoms. Well, we know that this isn't true. Besides, when sex educators present "success rates" of contraception, rather than emphasizing degrees of failure, they send the wrong signal to students. What parent would instruct his or her child, "By the way, if you ever decide to kill yourself, there's an 80% chance the bullet will be in another chamber?"

If you are not yet convinced that condoms are dangerous to the preservation of your life, let's take a look at what the medical field has to say? The following are testimonials from physicians on the effectiveness of condoms.

"Simply put, condoms fail. And condoms fail at a rate unacceptable for me as a physician to endorse them as a strategy to be promoted as meaningful AIDS protection."

Dr. Robert Renfield, chief of retro-viral research, Walter Reed Army Institute

"Relying on condoms for 'protection' can mean life long disease, suffering and even death for you and for someone you may love."

Dr. Andre Lafrance, Canadian physician and researcher

"Saying that the use of condoms is 'safe sex' is, in fact, playing Russian Roulette. A lot of people will die in this dangerous game."

Dr. Teresa Crenshaw, member of the U.S. Presidential AIDS Commission and past president of the American Association of Sex Educators

Pretty scary, isn't it? Good! It's supposed to scare you. It should scare you right out of someone else's bed and into a life of sexual purity where you belong.

Abortion

Pregnancy is a harsh reality that many young women are faced with considering that seventy-eight percent of their pregnancies are unplanned. One of the hardest decisions a college student must make is what to do: "Should I keep it or kill it?" For some women, abortion has become so normal that no real thought goes into the decision. There is no remorse or hesitation. Abortion is often seen as a normal procedure that must take place. If a college female has had one abortion, there is a strong likelihood that she'll have another. In fact, fifty-five percent of all women who have abortions are under 25 years of age are the largest percentage among college age women. So, for quite a few young adults, abortion is often used as a form of birth control.

Freshman women are the most likely candidates for unplanned pregnancy. An overwhelming number of freshman women don't know who the father of the unplanned child is because they've slept with so many people. Others, who are in relationships, abort because they're carrying some other man's baby. If they have the child they often don't return the following semester. These students either drop out of school or transfer to another school due to embarrassment. However, while many keep the child, even more choose to abort. The following is an account of a young college student's decision to terminate her pregnancy.

The bathroom was spinning like a crazed merry-go-round. The solid floor offered comfort to my bare feet, but none to my churning stomach. It felt like there was an alien trying to escape my body, but somehow it kept getting stuck in my throat. I knelt over the toilet, put one hand on the wall, and wrapped my arm around my waist like a seat belt. After three attempts, vomit finally bulldozed its way out, and I wearily flushed it down the toilet. I stumbled back to my room and searched for the calendar I used to track my periods. Reluctantly, I flipped through the calendar pages praying to see the red X indicating

October's monthly. But there was no X. I was late. I peeked into my T-shirt and stared down at my breasts, swollen like melons. For weeks, I never noticed how tender they were before. Maybe I did notice but refused to believe that I could be pregnant. During weeks of morning sickness, involuntary naps, and quarts of chocolate ice cream, I weighed the pros and cons of young unwed motherhood. I knew I wasn't mentally, spiritually, or financially prepared to raise a child. I refused to add another digit to the list of statistics about Black unwed mothers. I'm thankful Roe vs. Wade helped legalize abortion, so that I wouldn't have to suffer at the hands of back alley butchers as so many women from my own family and neighborhood have done.

While abortion is seen by many as a simple procedure to rid oneself of a problem, others have struggled with such a decision. Burdened with the thought of raising a child alone as well as the termination of an innocent fetus is a lot for a woman to endure. With the feeling of helplessness, many opt to terminate. Because of shame, abortion has always been a dirty little secret that many women have kept hidden in the innermost recesses of their minds hoping never to revisit again. A secret never told for fear of what others might think, say, or do. So, for years, women have hid behind numerous facades and false faces. Haunted by the memories of all that they've endured, they are forced to carry their past in their present.

Abortion clinics are constantly swarmed with angry protesters marching in sequence, holding signs and placards, chanting "Baby Killer!" and "Pro-life Not Pro-choice." Waiting rooms are packed with an array of hospital-gowned women consisting of: White married corporate executives, Black college students, Latina pre-teens accompanied by a parent and every other possible variation. The rooms are polluted with a loud deafening silence, periodically broken by the sounds of a sucking vacuum and an obscure cry from either the mother or the unborn child.

Women are called into the operating room every twenty-five minutes like clock- work. Lying face up on a flatbed with both legs outstretched in retractable stir-ups, women are forced to anxiously wait for the operation to begin. Momentarily met by a callous and discourteous physician, women are demanded to be still while the procedure takes place. While some women are completely sedated, others are partially conscious as they cry and hyperventilate while forced to witness the fetal extraction.

Once the procedure is complete, women are left on the operating table all alone. Immediately, two distinct feelings begin to take over the psyche of most women. While there is a feeling of relief, regret soon follows. Penetrating thoughts and suggestions begin to creep into their minds. "I'm so young to be doing things like this." "What if he never left me?" "I can never forgive myself for this?" Unfortunately, these thoughts never really go away. Periodically, many women have nightmares, waking up in cold sweats, haunted with the memory of a disfigured baby. Every year on the anniversary of the unborn child's would-be birthday, many women fall into a moderate or severe case of depression. "He would be three years-old now." "I wonder what he would have looked like." " I wonder what he would have been when he grew up?"

The traumatic experience of abortion may never be forgotten, but it can be forgiven. God is merciful enough to forgive you of your deed when you approach Him with a heart of repentance. A heart of repentance is remorse or self-reproach for what one has done or failed to do, resulting in a changed mind, heart and behavior.

So, for anyone reading this book faced with the difficult decision of what to do, the Bible provides an excellent plan of action:

"This day I call heaven and earth as witnesses against you that I have set before you life and death, blessings and curses, Now choose life, so that you and your children may live" Deut. 30:19 (TLB).

Black Beach Week

Every year, Black college students and other locals assemble for the most anticipated events of the year: Greekfest, Black Bike Week, Black Spring Break, The Cancun and Jamaica All-Star Festival, and many more. Tens of thousands of students all over the nation travel to engage in totally raw, wild and uncensored fun at some of the hottest *Black Beach Week* events in the country and throughout the world. The popularity of these events has also drawn television and radio personalities, pro-athletes, comedians, and national recording artists. The beach celebrations normally consist of dozens of parties, hour on the hour concerts, celebrity fashion shows, pajama and toga settings, parking lot pimpin', and an overwhelming ordeal of solicited sexual behavior.

Along the beach's boardwalk, tens of thousands of men and women walk up and down the strip from sun up to sun down. Women model scant, two-piece bathing suits, which they occasionally flash to gain the stares of men. Meanwhile, men walk around with video camcorders in search of the first sighting of bare feminine flesh they can find. Unfortunately, with explosive amounts of testosterone running rampant, many women are aggressively fondled and stripped of their suits by male brutes. Prostitutes perform public peep shows and erotic dances while being videotaped. Several men and women pose in erotic pictures, half dressed, while boldly grabbing each other's genitals; this occasionally leads to 'raw dog sex' (no condom) right in the middle of the street.

Beaches are continually absorbed with contests promoting promiscuity. While many free spirited women eagerly wait to be hosed down in wet T-shirt contests, others aggressively compete to be crowned queen of the banana sucking competition. Meanwhile, men indulge themselves in contests of their own. As bare women lather themselves in whipped cream, men venture to vigorously remove the palatable content with their tongues in record time. When the games are over, the top crest and throne are given to the most sexually carefree man and woman.

The Black Beach Party is a fantasyland for most. There are no parents, no professors and what appear to be no consequences. These three to seven days of pleasure have appropriately been labeled 'Sin Week'. Why? It's a secret world of drugs, alcohol and unrestrained orgasmic sex. It's a place of sexual free-for-alls and hard-core porn. People of all ages, from pre-teens to college students engage in group sex inside of pools, hotel rooms and street corners. Throughout the weekend, vendors unleash the uncut, unedited, straight off-the-meat-hook Black Beach tape and amateur porn video of the year. These tapes, which are shot exclusively for the fellas, contain some of the finest ladies, the smallest bikinis, the wildest shows and the rawest and most unbelievable footage ever caught on tape.

Whether in Cancun, Mexico, Antigua, Bahamas, Jamaica, or the States, an incalculable amount of students travel abroad for spring break with one reckless aim: to fulfill their most anticipated sexual fantasies. By the end of the week, most fantasies are fulfilled. However, while many claim to experience the greatest sexual thrill of their lives, there are countless students that return home with shattered dreams and in deep despair. They are forced to bear the sexual burdens and anxieties of the week. Some girls come back carrying the seed of a man she barely knew. Others leave being victims of rape and sodomy. Many return home infected with Herpes, Chlamydia, Syphilis, and HIV. And for what? A week of pleasure? They slept with strangers to satisfy their own sexual urges and now they will die with these strangers.

Gays, Lesbians & Bisexuals

Gay and lesbian organizations are now commonplace on college campuses. These organizations sponsor "Coming Out Week" where men and women admit their sexual preference. More and more students are admitting to being homosexual, lesbian and bisexual.

According to the *Details College Survey*, 64% of students support gay marriages. Even the majority of heterosexual undergraduate men, who tend to have the most conservative attitudes toward homosexual behavior, thought that gay marriage was acceptable, with 52% of them offering their support. Seventy percent of heterosexual women support gay marriage as well.

The college culture has changed so rapidly in its acceptance of homosexuality that many students who oppose the lifestyle are considered homophobic. Well, homophobia is defined as a persistent, abnormal or irrational fear of homosexuality. Therefore, disapproval does not constitute fear.

Whether in support or not, there are many who still have a very stereotypical view of homosexuals. Many envision very soft and flamboyant men with broken wrists, moist hands and relaxed or processed hair. Their mouths are contaminated with canker soars, their necks are covered with rash-like hickeys, and they speak with a high-pitched hiss, and pluralize every word. They don't just walk but they prance around in a vogue-like stride. While this image may serve someone's purpose, the reality is that there is no typical homosexual. Homosexuals come in all shapes, sizes and disguises.

Gay men are professors, they are football players, they are 'ruff necks'. They are the men who outwardly repudiate the homosexual lifestyle but clandestinely engage in homosexual rendezvous behind closed doors. They are the men in committed heterosexual relationships that secretly tiptoe into the dwellings of other men. They are everywhere, hiding behind the thick cloud of masculinity and manliness. They are men who would do anything to camouflage their true identity for fear of losing their families, their jobs and their reputations.

Likewise, lesbians are not just plain-faced, hard-core-butch types who wear short-cut naturals and boyish clothing. On the contrary, many are 'lipstick lesbians', very beautiful and feminine in nature. Interestingly, lesbians attribute the overall compassion and sensitivity of women to their sexual preference. They claim to share a deep connection with one another that can never be established with men. But sleeping with a woman doesn't guarantee anything. In Sister Souljah's book, *No Disrespect*, she states:

"Women, too can be power hungry exploiters. Women can also be two-time, low down cheats. Women can also be emotionally abusive and insensitive. Do not believe that same sex love will solve your problems. You can be hurt in any human relationship. Leaving your man because you have experienced pain, only to sleep with another woman will not guarantee that you will be treated more kindly, with greater tenderness, and with more respect. Women are abusers just like men. Confront your inner confusion before you enter into any relationship."

What is interesting is that Black men are more accepting of lesbian sex than they are of gay sex. There is just something kinky about seeing or thinking of two women having sex. But two men doing the "horizontal hokie-pokie" is disgusting. Despite such contrary thinking, perverted sex is perverted sex, whether it's two men or two women. The Bible clearly states its stance on homosexuality. In the book of Leviticus 18:22, the scripture states _"Homosexuality is absolutely forbidden, for it is an enormous sin"_(TLB).

What is also paradoxical is that people are more tolerant of same sex relationships than they are of interracial relationships. Many Black women will rant and rave about a brother dating some "stringy-haired white girl" and will fight tooth and nail to make him realize that he's made a mistake. However, some of her closest friends are brothers who date other men. But homosexual men are just as much of a threat as white women. They both contribute to the decreasing number of available men. However, while they cringe at interracial relationships, which aren't morally wrong, they support homosexual relationships, which are morally wrong.

The Prodigal Son That Never Returned

According to the _Details Magazine College Sex Survey_, the number one obstacle that college students face when engaging in sex is confronting their religious beliefs or personal value systems. As a result, many have replaced their association with organized religion for an obscure conceptualization of spirituality with no rules, commandments or laws to govern it. While many students profess to be spiritual, they continuously seek to satisfy the insatiable desires of their flesh. But sensuality has always been the biggest obstacle to spirituality because they are mutually exclusive. What's disturbing about the college experience is that many students who are sexually active are not aware of the spiritual tax that is involved in pre-marital sex. The deviation of many students' Biblical upbringing is reminiscent of the life-changing story of the 'Prodigal Son.'

A man had two sons. When the younger told his father, "I want my share of your estate now, instead of waiting until you die!" his father agreed to divide his wealth between his sons. A few days later this younger son packed all his belongings and took a trip to a distant land, and there wasted all his money on parties and prostitutes. About the time his money was gone a great famine swept over the land, and he began to starve. He persuaded a local farmer to hire him to feed his pigs. The boy became so hungry that even the pods he was feeding the swine looked good to him. And no one gave him anything. When he finally came to his senses, he said to himself, "At home even the hired men have food enough and to spare, and here I am, dying of hunger! I will go home to my father and say, 'Father, I have sinned against both heaven and you, and am no longer worthy of being called your son. Please take me on as a hired man.'" So he returned home to his father. And while he was still a long distance away, his father saw him coming, and was filled with loving pity and ran and embraced him and kissed him. His son said to him, "Father, I have sinned against heaven and you, and am not worthy of being called your son –"But his father said to the slaves, "Quick! Bring the finest robe in the house and put it on him. And a jeweled ring for his finger; and shoes! And kill the calf we have in the fattened pen. We must celebrate with a feast, for this son of mine was dead and has returned to life. He was lost and is found." So the party began.

Much like the 'Prodigal Son', Christian packed his bags, left home, and traveled to a distant land. Originally from a small town in the pastures of Arkansas, he moved to the big city of Atlanta, Georgia to attend school. Physically removed from the spiritual dwelling place of his youth, Christian was randomly placed deep within the erotic despotism of a campus dormitory. It was a dormitory full of strange customs, beliefs and behaviors. It was a dormitory laced with a universal creed echoed throughout the corridors of the building: 'If It Feels Good, Do It!'

Immediately uncomfortable with his new surroundings, Christian chose to spend most of his days in class or in the seclusion of his dorm room. Though the building he dwelled in was contaminated with the sexual sins of many students, Christian managed to successfully transform his dorm room into a sanctuary. On the outside of his door was a cross, signifying his Christian faith. His bookshelf was stacked with religious-based books and an assortment of various translation bibles. Above his bed was a picture of Christ praying at the mountain with his hands in a prayer posture. And under the picture was a caption that read "Live as though Christ died yesterday, rose today, and is coming tomorrow." Unfortunately, the moral-friendly environment that he created was not enough to keep him from falling into the temptations of a modern-day college campus.

Christian was a very handsome man and received the attention of many women, both on and off campus. His caramel skin, muscular build, curly hair, and hazel-brown eyes instantly put him in the category of 'Adonis.' Though strongly attracted to his physical make-up, most women were quite repulsed by his vow to celibacy. Even though many women claimed that sex didn't matter, they each knew they possessed something powerful enough to make him reconsider. They all said in the back of their perverse minds, "I'm gonna make this man lose his religion." However, Christian's relentless desire to stay sexually pure drove every flesh-hungry woman, desiring to get a taste, completely away. After weeks of women's unsuccessful pursuits for sexual ecstasy, Christian was spitefully nicknamed "The Untouchable."

But one woman who was able to successfully pierce through Christian's spiritual kryptonite into the innermost depths of his soul was D'Mona. She was his chemistry lab partner. D'Mona wasn't the most outwardly attractive woman on campus, but there was a strong sexual aura about her that overtook Christian every time he would lay eyes on her. Their partnership required that they spend time together outside of the classroom. Occasional phone calls and secluded study sessions afforded them the opportunity to get to know each other. Class reports and extensive lecture notes were frequently interrupted with intimate dialogue. The more familiar they became with each other, the less familiar they became with their work.

As one intense study session came to a close, Christian asked, "So, what time are we meeting tomorrow?" With a pause that left Christian in wonder, D'Mona slowly approached him as if she was planning to whisper something into his ear. Instead, to Christian's surprise, she cleverly slipped her body into his arms. Their eye contact was so intense, that a spoken word would ruin the visual exchange displayed between the two. With no thought to think, Christian hesitantly greeted D'Mona's welcoming mouth with his virgin lips. The pleasure of her soft skin left Christian in a somewhat eternal daze. But their moment of ecstasy would soon be interrupted with D'Mona's reply. "I'll see you tomorrow at 8 o'clock." She then disappeared into the empty halls of the college library.

With a strong sexual thirst for one another, their next meeting would be more intense than the first. Soon, the only course reviewed was the chemistry exchanged between the two. With a display of affection that could not be tolerated in public, meetings gradually moved from the library, to the residence hall, to Christian's dorm room. One night, D'Mona came to his room to study but deliberately left her books and notes at home. With a faint knock coming from the hallway, Christian expectantly opened the door. But, what met him at the door unleashed a desire that he never knew existed. D'Mona enticingly walked into the room with the sway of a runway model in slow motion. Immediately, Christian's eyes were lust-struck by her appearance. His nose inhaled the fruity fragrance delicately sprayed on her body. His mouth could taste the savory flavor of anticipation. With no more will to resist, Christian's hands began to slowly embrace the dimensions of her curvature frame.

As they stood in the guest area of the dorm, passionately kissing and caressing each other, D'Mona grabbed his hand and slowly led Christian into the bedroom. With his body ready to indulge in a sexual ecstasy never once experienced, his spirit began to speak to him. As he struggled to the bedroom, Proverbs 7:25-27 inconveniently arrested his mind: *"Let not your heart decline to her ways, go not astray in her paths, for she has cast down many wounded: yea, many strong men have been slain by her. Her house is the way to hell, going down to the chambers of death." (KJV)* Those sharp and powerful words pierced through his soul like a two-edged sword cutting into the lustful intents of his heart.

His mind was now warring with his flesh. Christian immediately pulled on D'Mona's arm and retreated from going into the bedroom. "Look, D'Mona, I don't think this is a good idea. We're moving way too fast." Without verbally responding to his hesitance, she slowly kissed him as she inched her way into the bedroom. Carefully laying him across his bed, D'Mona seductively responded, "I promise I won't do anything you don't want me to do." Naively, he believed her. She offered a massage and he accepted. Slowly, Christian's clothes began to peel piece by piece. The pinching, squeezing and grinding of her firm hands against his untouched back electrified his entire body. Without warning, Romans 8:13 shot through his mind like a piercing dagger. *"If you live to satisfy the lusts of your flesh, you will surely die."* Struggling with the power of God's words and the pleasure of D'Mona's warm embrace, he continued to lay there with his eyes closed, frozen in confusion.

Minutes later, he was awakened by a soft and warm body that straddled his lap. With one pull of his zipper, all hope was lost. D'Mona's seductive mastery was powerful enough to convince Christian to surrender his will. While engaged in the throes of passion, Christian occasionally glanced up at the portrait of Christ, perfectly placed along the wall above the center of his bed. And as he refocused on the intensity of the sexual act, Christian could feel the deep and penetrating stare of Christ's eyes, as though He were watching. All of a sudden, a clear voice spoke to him within the deep recesses of his mind. "Come back home, my son." Less than a minute later, that same virile voice said, "Come back home." Quickly turning back to the image of Christ, Christian's heart began to palpitate. Beads of sweat began to roll down his face. His muscles began to tense up. He cautioned D'Mona to stop. She complied. D'Mona noticed his worrisome state and decided to quickly dress herself and leave.

Once Christian heard the door slam, he broke out into tears. Wailing profusely, he began to cry out to God. The very bed that had been defiled became the very altar from which he would repent. Consumed with guilt and full of shame, Christian swore never to indulge in the forbidden pleasures of sex until the appointed time. For weeks, things were fine. There were no signs of lust lurking around, waiting to consume him. But Christian couldn't resist D'Mona's sexually suggestive speech. The sound of her voice coupled with the thoughts of that memorable night was too much for Christian to handle.

D'Mona convinced him to go back with her to the room after class. And, vulnerably, he followed her like an ox that follows a butcher to the slaughter waiting to be killed. Even though God chose to forget the sins of Christian's midnight rendezvous, his flesh could not resist the sexual sensation it craved for.

Now, back in the room, D'Mona began to tease Christian by slowly and enticingly peeling off her clothes. As each garment fell to the floor, his eyes became drunk with lust. In the fog of weakness, Christian wanted to resist, but hadn't the will to do so. He wanted to get up and leave but his feet wouldn't move. He wanted to run, and pitifully, he wanted to stay. But the moment she offered herself to him, he partook. Immediately, guilt, confusion, rationalization and despair hit Christian all at once. "How did I get myself into this? I can't believe I'm doing this. Uuuggghhh. But it feels so good." The more sex he had the less he would repent. Pretty soon, nothing could touch him. Sermons couldn't touch him. The portrait of Christ along the wall couldn't touch him. He asked God's forgiveness so often that he convinced himself that the well of mercy had run out.

Once again, in the heat of passion, he heard that familiar voice. "Come back home my son. You've gone too far and you've stayed too long." He wanted to stop, but he couldn't. The spirit of lust had consumed him. He wanted to do God's will, but there was something else deep within him that made him a slave to his weakness. As months went on, the more spiritually numb he became. Even though he declared he would one-day come back home, that day would never come.

On the eve of winter break, preparing to go home for the holidays, Christian and D'Mona attended a local college *Midnight Christmas Jam*. It was a night to remember. Santa was giving away gifts. Midgets were running around dressed like elves. People were kissing anywhere they found a mistletoe. Everyone was sipping on spiked eggnog. Christmas jingles were playing all throughout the night. Everyone was having a good time. Well, once the night came to an end, Christian and D'Mona got in the car and prepared to go back to the dorm for one last night of ecstasy before leaving to go back home. But, the anticipated sexual farewell never came.

Just minutes away from campus, Christian noticed a wavering object with blazing lights speedily approaching from a distance. Traveling down a dark, windy, country road, uncertain of the oncoming entity, he approached with caution. But no amount of prudence would be enough to avoid the inevitable catastrophe. Within seconds of identifying the oncoming object as a drunk-driven car, Christian saw his life flash before his eyes. Every sexual act and Godly warning deeply cut into his mind as the car made impact. The head-on collision instantly took lives. Shattered bones, splattered blood and disfigured bodies were among the remains. The body count was three. D'Mona and the drunk driver mysteriously survived. However, two passengers of the oncoming car and Christian were reported dead on arrival.

Christian would never have a chance to repent. He would never have an opportunity to come back home. He ignored the call of his Father. Christian had gone too far and stayed too long. Will you be the next Christian that will fall into the deplorable pit of sinful life? How many times have you ignored the call of your Father? How many times have you forcefully put the word of God in the deep recesses of your mind, in order to fulfill the lustful desires of your flesh? Christian didn't have a chance to repent. As a result, his eternity will be spent in hell. Why? The Bible is clear on its punishment for those who knowingly commit sin. Luke 12:47 says, *"He will be severely punished, for though he knew his duty he refused to do it."* It's one thing when you don't know the wrong that you do. But, when you knowingly do what is wrong, you're headed for disaster.

What did you do last year, last semester, or last night that you knowingly knew was wrong? The Bible says that anyone who knows the truth, but denies it, is like a man who looks in the mirror and, once he leaves, forgets what he looks like. So, if you know better, do better. It's a major struggle living on a college campus with an assortment of beautiful women and handsome men everywhere you turn. Believe me, I know. But there is a way that you can still keep your salvation without falling into the ditch. There is a three-step process for avoiding sexual temptation on campus:

1) Change Your Mind

Many Christian students lead a secret thought life of lust. These thoughts are either fantasies of sexual desires waiting to be fulfilled or reflections of sexual acts once performed. Well, these kinds of thoughts will lead one to sin. However, the Bible offers a simple two-step approach to overcoming a secret thought life. Second Corinthians 10:5 states, *"Casting down imaginations, and every high thing that exalteth itself against the knowledge of God, and bringing into captivity every thought to the obedience of Christ (KJV)."* Once evil thoughts are removed from your mind, they must be replaced with good thoughts. Philippians 4:8 states, *"Fix your thoughts on what is true and good and right. Think about things that are pure and lovely, and dwell on the fine, good things in others. Think about all you can praise God for and be glad about (TLB)."* Godly thoughts will produce godly behavior.

2) Change Your Relationships

Many Christians fall into sin because of the wrong associations. It is interesting how you can not personally benefit from someone's health, but their sickness is often contagious. Well, many people are spiritually sick and Christians are spiritually dying a slow death because of improper associations. The bible offers a clear solution to the problem. Second Corinthians 6:14-15 states *"Don't be teamed with those who do not love the Lord, for what do the people of God have in common with the people of sin? How can light live with darkness? And what harmony can there be between Christ and the devil? How can a Christian be a partner with one who doesn't believe? (TLB).* If you are personally struggling with letting go of certain associations, just remember this one thing. If you can't change the friends you're around, change the friends you're around.

3) Change Your Environment

College parties, clubs, and other social and private events with a heavy influence of drugs, alcohol and sex may not be a healthy place to be. No matter how strong you may think you are, there is always something that can cause you to stumble. Christians that think they are strong enough are usually the first to fall into the ditch. Join a local church or a Bible-study group on campus. The presence of other Christians is the most edifying environment for your mind, spirit and body. God has a dwelling place for you. Ephesians 2:19 states, *"Now you are no longer strangers to God and foreigners to heaven, but you are members of God's very own family, citizens of God's country, and you belong in God's household with every other Christian (TLB)."*

The application of these three simple steps will put you on the path of a sexually pure college experience. College was designed as place to receive an education that would aid in furthering one's personal and professional advancement. It was not designed to 'get your freak on' with someone that seems pleasing to the eye. So, to all of you horny college students that daily crave to fulfill the lustful desires of your flesh, do like mama used to say: "Ladies, keep your panties up and your legs closed. Gentlemen, keep it zipped up." If students can grab hold of this one principle, much of their behavior will be pleasing in the sight of God.

Black Guys

An intimate touch was not enough
As I ask myself the question
Oh how did this lust affair begin
My flesh lusts against my spirit
And my spirit against my flesh
For I am weak
As I seek to find a virtuous woman
But am I a righteous man
Countless times I've spent with illegitimate mates
That I've replaced
One after another
Life...full of games
And for what
A moment of fortune and fame
Unwarranted sex, lies, cheap thrills...
How many raw deals
Will I make for the sake of my soul
Pressured by the voices in my head
To repent for the sins that I commit
A high price I sacrifice...for lust
In God I trust
So I must release my secret sins from within.

Black Thighs
Black Guys
&
Bedroom Lies

The Game

Meeting In My Bedroom

School Days

Somebody's Sleeping In My Bed

Whatever Happened to Black Love?

Don't Wanna Be A Playa No More

Good Lovin'

Chapter Four

SOMEBODY'S SLEEPING IN MY BED

The violation happened in an instant, but festered over the course of time. Resentment, acts of rage, regret and utter chaos consumed their almost depleted relationship. The thin battle line between love and hate was laid. Weapons were drawn and all-out war was waged. Shattered glass, broken appliances, tattered clothing and verbal venom were the least of their concerns. The poisonous relationship often got progressively worse. But nothing would top the day Jason held Monique hostage within the confines of her own home.

Trapped in her one-bedroom apartment, bound by the verbal shackles of Jason's threats, Monique helplessly screamed,

"Let me go!" With absolutely no intention to comply, Jason quickly and possessively responded, "No, uh uh! I told you before; you ain't goin' nowhere. I'm not gonna let you leave me." Physically blocking the door after ripping the phone jack out of the wall, Jason refused to let her leave until their relationship was restored. "Restored back to what?" Monique asked. "It's over, o.k! I trusted you. I loved you. But you betrayed me! And there ain't nothin' to restore. So, let me go!" Filled with a stubbornness that wouldn't take no for an answer, Jason forcefully grabbed Monique in an act of desperation. "I told you it's not over between us. So just calm down so we can talk about this. Don't make me hurt you." Struggling to free herself from his death clutch, Monique responded, "Get off of me! I can't stand you! You ain't no man! You ain't nothin' but a punk. I hope you catch a disease, die and go to hell!"

Monique's words were like daggers that pierced into Jason's ego. Verbally paralyzed by her vicious attack, Jason stood in front of Monique boiling with rage. The left side of his upper lip began to twitch with disgust. His eyes turned red with the blood of revenge and a vein popped out of the side of his forehead as beads of sweat fell from his face. Left mentally challenged, with no words to retaliate, Jason grabbed Monique by the throat with an attempt to squeeze the life out of her. Throwing her up against the bedroom wall, Jason yelled, "I'll kill you, girl. Don't you ever, ever disrespect me like that again. I'll kill you, Monique!" Straining to take another breath, Monique did the only thing she knew how to do. She kicked Jason in the very place that was used to sexually satisfy another woman. Jason fell to the ground agonizing from the razor-sharp pain, while gasping for the air that was lost with the swiftness of one kick. Immediately, Monique ran for the door with tears streaming down her face and the indents of handprints wrapped around her neck. Hesitantly returning hours later, Jason was no where to be found. He left her apartment never to return again.

This tragic ending was the result of a tragic set of circumstances. You see, Jason willingly partook of the forbidden fruit of another woman. It was his admittance of a single act of infidelity that drove Monique over the edge. His long awaited confession of past sexual indiscretions and the circumstances that followed led to the death of their relationship. What an unfortunate set of circumstances they were.

It all began in the summer of '98. Monique was a third-year student at the University of Delaware. Her outstanding academic performance awarded her a summer internship with the Pharmacology department at the University of Maryland at Baltimore. It was in Baltimore that she met Jason through a mutual friend. The attraction was strong and they hit it off right away. Although Monique's focus was directed on a summer's workload of prostate cancer research, Jason's companionship made her temporary stay all the more pleasurable.

The remaining weeks were filled with elaborate conversations, countless dates and sexual ecstasy. By the end of the summer, Jason and Monique made arrangements of how they would successfully continue their newfound relationship.

The first few months consisted of written letters and continuous phone calls. But it wasn't long before such communication would leave them both emotionally and sexually unfulfilled. During Monique's Fall break, she made plans to visit Jason for the weekend. The passionate weekend was followed by a return visit the very next month. After continuous trips to Baltimore, Monique frequently questioned when Jason would finally pay her a visit. That time soon came, but it was more than what she bargained for.

Jason's arrival was well received by several women on campus. During his four-day stay, women on campus murmured amongst themselves, "Ooh, whose man is that?" "Girl, he is so fine!" "Monique betta' watch her man before somebody takes him." These remarks persisted until the end of his stay. However, one woman who undoubtedly had a strong attraction for Jason, went beyond mere words. Subtle body language and inviting gestures were her methods of catching Jason's eye. Shannika was known for stealing other women's men. She had already done it twice that semester and Jason was next on her list. Monique knew how scandalous Shannika could be and never liked her. She swore that if Shannika even looked at her man, it would be on. Fortunately, his visit was without incident.

However, as time went on things began to change. The laughter and chatter of another man in the background often interrupted Jason's calls. Every time he inquired about the guy in her room, Monique attempted to assure him that it was her roommate's boyfriend. Uneasy to convince, Jason got madder by the minute. Phone calls often escalated into heated arguments. "Tell that nigga to get out of your room", Jason yelled. "I told you already, I'm not doing anything. He's my roommate's boyfriend and he's always in here. I can't just tell him to leave." Jason wasn't convinced and insisted that Monique was cheating on him. Nothing she said could assure Jason of her commitment to him. As months went on, he became more jealous and resentful. He would visit without warning. His phone calls became very sporadic and his behavior, inconsistent. Jason convinced Monique to move off campus into a one-bedroom apartment to assure him of her faithfulness. Jason even insisted on relocating and moving in with her.

Once the transition was made, things got progressively better. All of Jason's doubts were resolved. However, Monique's proven commitment left him burdened with guilt. The more Monique expressed her love for Jason, the worse he felt. Everything inside of him wanted to confess, but his lips wouldn't agree with what his mind was telling him to do. But the more she did for him, the more compelled he was to reveal the truth.

One night, after a very intense sex session, Jason sat on the edge of the bed, with his back turned towards her, and said, "Monique, there's something I have to tell you. I know you're gonna hate me for this. But I can't keep this thing hidden anymore. I slept with Shannika out of revenge because I thought that you were cheating on me." Silence consumed the room. As he turned toward her in wonderment, all he could see was the blank expression on her face. Monique spoke not another word that night. In fact, many nights were consumed with dead air. Flowers, candy, apologetic notes around the house and the shedding of tears couldn't make up for what he did. There was something Jason didn't understand. Not only was Monique enraged by what he did, but with whom he did it with. To know that he'd slept with

Shannika was too much for Monique to handle. The love that she once felt turned to contempt.

After a month of begging and pleading, Monique's vulnerability began to kick in. Finally giving in to Jason's heart-felt apologies, the night was spent rekindling what was lost through the highest form of physical expression. It was gentle, pleasurable and a completely beautiful experience. Monique cried from start to finish. It appeared as if things were getting better. However, things took a turn for the worst. Three days later, Jason told Monique that Shannika was two months pregnant and refused to abort it. "What?" Monique helplessly asked. "You got that tramp pregnant? I don't believe this!" Tension mounted. Hits were exchanged. Egos were hurt. The belligerent exchange continued for several weeks, but no word or physical blow could equal the torment that was felt when Monique discovered that she was two weeks late. Her period had not yet come. Frantically checking her calendar and realizing that no condom was used that night, Monique quickly decided that an abortion was the only option. She refused to have Jason's baby. He did everything to convince her otherwise, but she refused. Her clinical appointment was made and there was no turning back.

Lying on the cold operating table, completely sedated, the doctor began to perform the procedure. However, minutes into the operation he noticed something very alarming and suspended the surgery. He quickly dressed Monique and walked her out to the waiting room to inform both her and her family that she was pregnant with twins and should reconsider. Barely conscious enough to make an informed decision, Monique slurred, "How much more will it cost?" Despite Jason's opposition to proceed, Monique's mother and sister immediately scraped together the additional amount the doctor quoted.

Once the procedure was complete, Jason took Monique's car and attended Shannika's baby shower held in the campus student center for all to see. Shannika wanted the campus to know that Monique's boyfriend was her baby's daddy. Jason left his girlfriend lying unconscious on an operating table to celebrate the child of his closet-freak lover. Monique felt that Jason's actions were the most degradable thing that he could have ever done to her. Not only did Jason ruin Monique's life, but he also made her the laughing stock of the campus. She would always be known as the girl who couldn't keep her man and Shannika's protruding stomach was a constant reminder of that. Every time Monique laid eyes on Shannika, her hatred for Jason intensified. Monique was now at her wits end.

The next morning, before leaving for class, Monique woke Jason up and informed him that the relationship was over and that he had to get out. "I don't care where you go, but you gotta get out of here", said Monique. "Whatcha' mean get out?" Jason surprisingly asked. "I'm not going anywhere and neither are you." Their verbal exchange and Monique's temporary captivity led to the beginning of the end of their relationship.

One partner's burden of insecurity resulted in a senseless act of revenge, or spite-sex, which destroyed a relationship, a reputation and innocent lives yet unborn. How many of you reading this book, whether married or single, have meddled in the affairs of the forbidden. How many hearts have you broken? How many families have you destroyed? How many casualties have you caused through the selfish act of infidelity? Before you answer, keep reading.

What Is Infidelity?

Infidelity is simply defined as unfaithfulness, betrayal or lack of loyalty to a spouse or partner. Unfortunately, many people believe that, as long as a relationship is not physically consummated, it can't be considered infidelity. This belief is totally erroneous. Infidelity can begin at the point of a strong emotional connection—making infidelity both sexual and emotional. Infidelity can be a heightened emotional connection, as well as a sexual longing for someone other than your partner.

According to a 1997 University of Chicago study, seventy-eight percent of Americans admit that cheating is wrong. Most relationships are affected by this heinous act. In the 1999 movie release, *The Best Man*, the character Lance, played by Morris

Chestnut, expressed his very naïve views on marriage as he and his groomsmen sat around the table playing cards. He expressed, "Marriage is gonna curb that appetite for more women. In case you didn't know, marriage is the cure to promiscuity." Though it may sound good, his statement is emphatically wrong.

The *1993 Janus Report on Sexual Behavior* bills itself as "The First Broad-Scale Scientific National Survey since Kinsey." Its research concludes that one in three married men and one in four married women have had at least one extra-marital affair. This amounts to a lot of people engaging in infidelity. Dr. Stateli claims that 60 percent of all marriages are touched by extra-marital affairs, with approximately 50% of married men and almost 40% of married women who commit adultery. Similarly, the psychologist Dr. Bonnie Euker Weil in her book *Adultery: The Forgivable Sin (1994)* estimates that 85 percent of all marriages will be touched by infidelity. Also, 60 percent of all single men and women have had an intimate relationship with a married person.

However, most information gathered on infidelity comes from data collected on married couples. It's not restricted to the husband or wife with a seven-year itch. It seems if so many people will violate their marriage vows, the number of extra sexual affairs in dating relationships must be even higher. Inversely, most people who cheat before marriage will cheat after marriage and people who've had many sexual partners are more likely to cheat during marriage.

A majority of young adult relationships have been characterized by betrayal on the part of somebody in the relationship. More than 60% of college-aged students have experienced sexual betrayal, according to S. Shirley Feldman, senior research scientist in the Division of Child and Adolescent Psychiatry and Child Development. Sixty-one percent of students reported that they have been unfaithful (kissing, petting, sexual intercourse, spending time with another, becoming emotionally close to another) in their current relationship. So, for most students, monogamy is a theory that is not widely practiced on a college campus.

Infidelity has occurred with such frequency that it's the rule rather than the exception. Because of the excessiveness of the act, many couples have worked out ground rules for permissible extra-sexual affairs. There are prostitutes, both male and female, who are granted sexual exception when it is done for business rather than pleasure. Swingers encourage mate swapping and orgies as long as the sex is performed in public, but are outraged over private intimacies. Travelers have permission to indulge in extra sexual affairs when outside of city limits, or in one case, more than a four-hour drive from home. In some relationships men are given the privilege to have affairs while women aren't. It's justified by maintaining that men can have affairs casually, while women are in danger of becoming romantically involved.

Even though couples have made provisions for infidelity in their relationships, these forms of extra-sexual arrangements are quite rare. Most affairs are kept hidden in secrecy. Flirtation that goes too far leads to private meetings, secret promises, broken agreements, damaging revelations, and self-deception. Sexual perpetrators are usually guilty of telling one lie to cover up another. Their workings are very clandestine. They sneak around hoping never to be caught. It's the secrecy that becomes part of the overall excitement. The danger of being busted can be as pulse tingling as the new relationship itself. It adds spice to life in the midst of a bland relationship.

So, why not just leave the relationship? Many married adulterers claim leaving would cause too much of a financial burden for the rest of their lives. Many stay because kids are involved. Many couples remain together, bound by children not love. Alimony, child support, and lawyer fees can get pretty expensive. Many non-married couples stay for convenience and genuine care for one another, despite their scandalous behavior.

Meanwhile, the relationship dies a slow death. The dishonesty that is necessary to sustain an affair is what hurts people the most. Trying to live with lies, half-truths, cover-ups, and deceit leads to a disturbing sense of guilt that eats away at one's conscience like a parasite. Insecurity and paranoia are also two of the many results of cheating. Most people who cheat start to question the loyalty of their partner because they assume that the very thing that they've done is being done to them.

The victims of infidelity suffer as well. Many of these individuals value their body and believe in monogamy. To them, infidelity is an unforgivable sin and is the epitome of betrayal. To them, sex and love are not mutually exclusive. Rather, they are one in the same. The betrayal often leaves them irate with anger not easily understood. They often feel cheap, dirty and completely humiliated. The victim normally initiates venomous insults, raging tears and ferocious attacks. By then, the victim is ready to kill. The relationship is severely threatened.

Infidelity is a selfish act that provides a feeling of instant gratification. However, the long-term results are normally detrimental. It is venom that poisons relationships. It is a heinous act that fosters resentment, bitterness, distrust, and animosity between two individuals. If this poisonous venom is not neutralized with a mutual commitment to monogamy, relationships will continue to die a slow and agonizing death.

Why Men Cheat

Cheating is nothing new for men in this society. Experts have gathered that a disturbing seventy-five percent of married men or men involved in serious relationships cheat. In many cases, sex and love have always remained two separate issues for men. Affairs are initiated for sex and long-term relationships are endured for love. While he genuinely needs the comfort that his primary relationship gives him, he is not willing to give up his sexual liaison. Sexual betrayal can involve kissing, petting or intercourse with a non-partner. Many men may chose to indulge in sexual play, void of intercourse, and convince themselves that they're not cheating.

Larry was in a two-year monogamous relationship until he met Donna. He loved Leshaun, his girlfriend, but couldn't resist his physical attraction to Donna. They started seeing each other regularly. Their meetings always escalated into something very physical. But, no matter how intense things got between them in the bedroom, Larry always bailed out just before the point of penetration. They'd kiss, fondle, and even have oral sex, which often drove them to orgasm. But, every time Donna straddled his lap, he would push her away. He would often tell her that he didn't want to cheat on his girlfriend, which embittered Donna. After a pattern of foul play on Larry's part, Donna decided to leave the relationship because she realized that their interaction was just an opportunity for him to have guilt-free oral sex.

When a man is unfaithful, he will seldom confess. Generally, he has to get caught. Even when he is caught red-handed, he will often try to lie his way out of it. This is why many men prefer sex with no strings attached. It is this kind of extra-sexual affair that is often anonymous and uncomplicated. Perhaps only first names get exchanged. Rarely are addresses or personal histories discussed. And the partners walk away from their liaison with nothing given and nothing received except the pleasure of their time in bed. This is the classic one-night stand.

Men also enter into long-term relationships that may prove to be more complicated to maintain. However, technological devices such as pagers, cell phones, voice mail and e-mail, make it far less risky of being caught. Whether men are looking for temporary thrills or long-term extra-sexual relationships, it all adds up to one thing: cheating. And their reasons often vary. The following reasons for infidelity are widely expressed by men.

Women Stand For It

Experts say men wouldn't cheat if women didn't let them. Women marry men who have cheated on them during their relationship expecting things to change with a newfound commitment. However, a man who has cheated on his girlfriend or fiancée will probably cheat on his wife. Once the discovery of infidelity is made, many women continue to stay. Some women, desperate to stay in the relationship have agreed, " I'd rather lie down next to a cheater than no man at all. At least I know where he's at and whom he's with. This attitude allows a man to continually cheat with no remorse.

Thrill Seeking
Men often suffer from boredom in their relationships. After the newness has worn off, things that were once exciting become dry. The emotional and sexual connection between partners is replaced by the realties of everyday life. In order to break away from this mundane lifestyle, men seek undercover lovers, hoping to obtain a feeling that is no longer present in his current relationship. They both aim to satisfy each other mentally and physically. The thrill of possibly getting caught by a spouse and the adventures of the forbidden bring a level of excitement back into his life.

Don Juanism
Some men have a compulsive need to engage in several sexual experiences. These experiences are void of emotion or romance. It's simply satisfying a craving for sex. They are sexual opportunists. They feel compelled to find someone to sexually conquer. They spend time scheming of ways to get into a woman's bed. And once the act is over, they leave. They continue to be driven by the thrill of a new body, the excitement of a new challenge and hearing a different set of moans and groans.

John 32, engaged
"I often go straight from my lover's bed to my fiancée's. It's a real turn on for me to have been with someone else and then make love to my lady as soon as I get home. Having sex with one woman is much too difficult when there are so many out there to choose from. As soon as I'm finish with one, I find someone else that I've got to have. I don't know, I guess I'm just addicted to a pretty face, soft skin and a banging body."

Ego boost
Many men look for reassurance of their manhood from other women. Ironically, just like women, men seek self-worth and self-esteem in their relationship. They constantly have to have their egos stroked. They want to know that they've still got it. So, if they can't get that assurance from their partner, they'll get it from a secret lover. While men's self-worth may erode in the relationship,

they are often told how wonderful, sexy, loving and understanding they are by their lover.

Seeking revenge
Men may often seek revenge in their relationships as a justifiable means of getting back at their partner for something said or done, whether sexual or non-sexual. He may feel she only cares about his money. He may think she's too critical. He may be under the brunt of attack and constantly disrespected in private and public. Whatever the reason, he feels cheating will balance the scale in the relationship. Although he assumes his partner will never discover his indiscretions, simply knowing how much it would hurt her if she did know is enough to satisfy him.

Sexual Frustration
Many men may complain of too little sex or routine sex in the relationships. Unfortunately, these men judge their sex life by how many weekly encounters they have. These men often want more frequent sex, better sex or different sexual experiences. The same routine sexual encounter is seen as boring. There is nothing new or exciting about it. It's dull and unrewarding. Therefore, if their sexual needs aren't met, they will seek a partner outside of their relationship who is more willing to experiment and try new things.

Relationship Frustration
Men often feel unappreciated and disrespected by their partner. Constantly assaulted by complaints and mean-spirited words, many men are tempted to go where they are appreciated. This is when other women, who notice their finer qualities, become enticing. Relationship drama often serves to push men further and further away until they wind up in the arms of another woman. Therefore, a need for admiration may often turn into an emotional as well as sexual affair.

Why Women Cheat

Though cheating has exclusively been deemed a male phenomenon, more and more women are getting caught with their hands in the cookie jar as well. Polls show that forty-five to fifty-five percent of all married women would be unfaithful by age forty. If approximately forty percent of wives in this country have extra-marital relationships that would mean twenty-one million wives have sampled the pleasures and pains of a secret love life. A 1997 Ball State University study suggests that young women under the age of 40 are just as likely to commit adultery as men their age. Shocking, isn't it?

Lacking discretion, many women brag about their infidelity. They boast about sexing down a man they have on the side and then going home to squeeze in a sex session with their husband or boyfriend later that same day. They laugh about how they've been able to get away with their schemes for so long. Radio programs, newspaper columns and magazine articles provide safe and anonymous outlets for women to confess their indiscretions. One woman tells her story in the March 2000 edition of *Women's Own Magazine*. She says:

"Remember Gary, Well, I slept with him. Ian and I were at their house on Sunday and we were all dipping in the champagne and swimming in their pool. Ian went off to buy some booze and Gary's wife said she wanted to see a friend who was sick. It was just Gary and I in the pool. We started flirting and then he kissed me. I think I knew it was coming but I was still surprised. He slipped his fingers inside my swimsuit and I was gone. The next minute we were frantically sexing on the side of the pool, and I climaxed in about one minute flat. I felt guilty. I've now betrayed Ian in reality, not just in my head. Gary called me at work today and said he was sorry. I don't want him to be sorry. I wanted more, and I told him so. I still feel guilty, but if Ian's not going to satisfy me, he can't expect me to be faithful. I feel resentful that we've slipped into "extra-marital sex" since we've only been married for a year. I have no idea what will happen now that I'm having an affair, but at least Gary's good in bed."

Sounds pretty cold. But, are women cheating for cheating sake? It's possible. However, cheating normally indicates that there are problems in the relationship. Though there is no moral justification for cheating, women have strayed from the sanctity of their relationships for various reasons.

Self-Esteem Boost

Women have a compelling need to always feel beautiful, sexy and desirable. They want and need to know that someone loves them for who they are, rather than for the successful completion of tasks, duties and responsibilities. They need to know that someone supports their dreams and most intimate desires. Unfortunately, countless boyfriends and husbands show little interest in their personal and relational fulfillment. This causes women to seek assurance outside of their relationships.

Revenge

After finding lipstick stains on shirt collars, different color panties hidden in closets and unfamiliar condoms in back seat pockets, a woman can become irate. Such betrayal brings the worst out of many, especially if they have been faithful and devoted. These women will seek revenge and embark upon an affair of their own in response to their partner's indiscretions. This is also known as spite sex. It's simply used to strike back at the partner. However, many women admit that the sweetest revenge is when they keep their affairs secret.

Seeking Excitement

When a relationship has reached its peek and normalcy sets in, many women strive to keep the thrill and excitement alive. If the relationship can't be revived, they'll find it somewhere else. Though they love their significant other and would never consider leaving, they often become tired of the monotony of the relationship. You know: the daily six o'clock meal, the Tuesday-night-only sex session, and the weekend house cleaning. Everything has become stale and predictable, and predictability leads to "yawnability." So, many women will go outside of their relationships to find that spark and excitement.

Seduction and Romance
Men haven't understood that the way that you get a woman is the same way you have to keep a woman. Men typically romance women right into a relationship. However, once their spot is secured, the romance slowly wanes into oblivion. This often creates a serious problem because women want to continue being wined and dined, courted and romanced. Anytime a man fails to compliment, care for and pamper his woman—she will find someone who will. He may not notice her new dress, new hairstyle or sweet smelling perfume, but someone outside that relationship will. After time, she looks forward to the compliments, phone calls and flowers and candy provided by the other man. Not only is he sweet to her, but he listens too. While her conversation with her significant other is typically stale, the dialogue she shares with the other man brings her life. Then she begins comparing the other man to her man: "Why can't he be more attentive and supportive?" This scenario often leads to an adulterous affair. One woman offers her personal testimony.

Dawn, 28, married
"It was at a vulnerable point in my marriage when I got involved with my lover. My husband and I weren't getting along. I was getting a lot of negative things thrown at me and my lover kept giving me positives. He was always complimenting me and seemed to understand when my husband did not. I don't know what my hopes are for the future. When my husband and I are getting along I feel a tremendous amount of guilt. When we don't get along. I then understand why I am doing what I am doing."

Genuine Friendship
Many women are led into an affair through the pull of friendship. Feeling that something is wrong or missing in their relationship, they try to compensate for it by taking on a lover. Women have affairs when they find someone they can relate to emotionally, a man who seems to understand and accept them just as they are. Many women have been lured into a strange bed because of their ability to let their guards down. They feel good being able to talk to and confide in their lovers.

101

Sugar-Daddy Search
Regardless of how much her husband or boyfriend financially provides in the relationship, it's never enough. This type of woman is attracted to men with money, power and position. She's attracted to what he is, not who he is. When this woman has an affair, it has a lot to do with the social and financial status that goes along with the association.

In the June '98 edition of *Just For Black Men* magazine, Jay Cash wrote an interesting article entitled, 'Is There Such A Thing As Justified Cheating?' Many brothers and sisters agree that there are justifiable reasons for cheating in relationships. Most of the scenarios provided in the article pertained to emotional and sexual inadequacy. One case, however, dealt specifically with finances.

"Debra Harrison, an attractive secretary from Washington, D.C. says, "ain't nothing going on in her life but the rent." She requires any man she involves herself with to be well paid, thus having more money to maintain her. However, she recently fell for a brother named Darryl, who made less money than she did. She liked Darryl a lot, but not nearly as much as he liked her. He had fallen in love with her. He had everything she wanted in a man, except money. He treated her like no man had ever treated her. She felt special, desired and appreciated. But something was not right. Then she figured it out. Her bills weren't getting paid."

Sexual Deprivation
Some women simply cheat for sex. Men and women reach sexual peaks at different times. Women normally peak much later than men do. So, when she wants sex, he doesn't. Some men can't sexually perform as vigorously because their testosterone level drops. As a result, their sexual performance decreases. They'd rather not have sex than be embarrassed. Meanwhile, women are left sexless. They feel as if they are left with no other option than to seek sexual fulfillment outside the relationship.

Infidelity In The Workplace

The workplace has recently become the latest hot spot for infidelity. It's has transformed into a sexy place. With more women obtaining positions in 'Corporate America' in record numbers, more men and women have been placed in direct contact with one another on a daily basis. After eight long hours of light conversation and frequent interaction, many things are bound to occur. In time, an innocent proposal for lunch can turn into a lunch 'quickie'.

Since the initial advancement of women in the workforce, Carol Tavis and Susan Sadd, reporting on the sex lives of one hundred thousand women, found that forty-seven percent of wives employed full-time had been unfaithful by the age of forty' compared to the thirty-three percent of housewives. Literally one out of three women have found a secret lover in the workplace.

During an intense interview one woman admitted that she frequently comes to work with no underwear on which teases and drives her lover wild. The woman states: "Sex at lunch-time can be not only exciting, but romantic. The only problem is figuring out where to have it. Doing it behind the photocopier, on top of your boss' desk, in parking lots, inside cubicles, in elevators, in empty stairwells, and in other areas in the office can be very risky. But the risk of getting caught can make it the best sex you ever had. But the best part is having sex during lunch and coming back to the office acting very professional and businesslike."

The reasons why people cleverly turn boardrooms into bedrooms vary. Couples often work inordinately long hours apart from each other from the moment they leave for work until the time they crawl into bed. They may work different shifts. While one partner is snuggled in the comfort of a bed, the other is burning the midnight oil on the job. There are many relationships that endure the burden of excessive travel. While one partner is home sleeping in an empty bed, the other is somewhere far off in a hotel room. These awkward circumstances leave a lot of room for infidelity.

Many people cheat with a purpose. Some women cheat for professional or social advancement. A woman admits, "I guess I was sleeping my way to the top. I knew it was wrong, but at the same time I felt I would never get my career going if I didn't. What I didn't expect was the effect it had on other parts of my life. I thought my husband would never suspect. Unfortunately, he did, and he was so angry he filed for divorce." Though troubling, women are not alone.

Businessmen who frequently travel attending conventions say that these temporary homes-away-from-home, with their abundance of alcohol, corporate-sponsored social gatherings and pampered surroundings virtually amount to a petri dish of passion. Meanwhile, the wife is at home allowing another man to help her keep her sheets warm until her husband returns.

Out of the thousands of responses to an informal *Travel & Leisure* magazine travel survey in 1999, more than one in five said they had a convention fling. That's just those who admit to it. "People think of business conferences as summer camp for grown-ups", says Pepper Schwartz, sociology professor at the University of Washington. "They're thrown together in a kind of semi-holiday mood. There is a lot of intimacy-building moments, like going out to dinner and talking about work you care passionately about. Seeing somebody whose expertise makes you admire them, makes you want to know them better."

While many people are having sexual rendezvous in corporate offices, others are going on sexual excursions at conventions. Some are glued to their seats initiating two-timing exchanges over a keyboard while their real-life romances suffer. Internet infidelity is far more widespread than ever. People are involved in online affairs for the same reasons people engage in extra-marital affairs: they are trying to meet needs that are not being met within their relationships.

The Internet has made infidelity more easily accessible. A person no longer has to creep out of the house and fear being seen by friends, family, colleagues or church members. Though there is no physical contact, two individuals can still engage in sex online. It's cyber sex. Sharing erotic thoughts with another person resulting in masturbation is what makes these exchanges adulterous. It's amazing how the Internet has become a growing threat to the stability of relationships. Though the affair may never progress beyond the keyboard, most spouses feel betrayed. While men limit the experience to an innocent sexual daydream shared with another person, the unbearable feeling of jealousy grips the hearts of women.

A Cheat-Driven Society

Most people were taught how to commit infidelity. Society, mass media and just about every dimwitted "expert" or psychologist has proclaimed that monogamy is impossible in today's world and that sexual exclusivity is archaic. Doctors state that humans aren't biologically monogamous. Books have even been written which counsel its readers on how to have successful affairs.

The media glorifies infidelity with absolutely no consequences. From talk shows, to soap operas, to weekly sitcoms--cheating is familiar and acceptable behavior. Televised comedians have incorporated a humorous acceptance of infidelity in their stand-up routines. Daily late-night radio programs and relationship magazines are full of anonymous confessions of sexual foul play. Motion pictures have even joined the group in its vivid portrayals of infidelity.

Terrence Howard's character, Quentin, in *The Best Man*, asserts his opinion of infidelity. "Ain't nothing natural about no monogamy. I mean, God did not intend for us to be with just one person. If he had, He wouldn't have given us all this sperm and these b---hes would not out number us the way that they do." Even though the other male characters jovially laughed it off, countless men fully endorse his philosophy.

Bill Bellamy's debut film, *How To Be A Playa*, is a step-by-step depiction of sexual affairs, acting as a how-to guide for cheating. The entire movie is centered on a day in the life of Bellamy's character Dre, who clandestinely roams around town indulging in numerous sex sessions with various women while assuring Lisa, his girlfriend, of his commitment. Dre's three friends, whom he gives cardinal rules of how to be a playa, accompany his journey.

Hopping from home to home, Dre is met by Barbara, an aerobics instructor from the top floor of his apartment building. He then visits Amber, a white woman who executes sexual role-playing performances. Dre routinely meets Sherry, an animalistic nymphomaniac, who unveils whips, chains and dildos during foreplay. Dre then drops by Robin's home, a housewife, to indulge in quickie-sex, which is later discovered by her husband. Sherry, a Jamaican diva, and Cece, a spaced-out psychedelic, are also among Dre's erotic excursions. Claiming to be the player of all players, he is set-up and finally busted in his adulterous act by his girlfriend Lisa. Though the movie ended with the discovery of his illicit affair, men and women left the theater with new schemes and plots of how to perfect their undercover extra-sexual affairs.

Rural and downtown areas are infested with strip joints and gentlemen's clubs that give men and women the option to tiptoe out of their relationships in order to fulfill the lustful desires of their hearts. These bars are filled with male and female strippers who depend on their bodies and the ability to separate people from money. 'Lap dances' are performed with the intention of bringing men to orgasm. Penal grinding is performed on women for the purpose of female arousal. Though sex is not carried out, these casual visitations act as non-sexual one-night stands. Society has become so bombarded with infidelity that many have lost hope in humanity.

Carmen, 23, Single
"There's no such thing as a cheat-free relationship because the media has made it too popular and acceptable. And it's easy to get away with. All you have to do is just apologize. The very ones who I thought had a great sense of integrity, were the very ones that wound up cheating."

Countless men and women share this belief. For this reason, many expect their relationships to be contaminated by the practice of infidelity. Several people avoid relationships all together for fear of the inevitable. Unfortunately, the world views monogamy as a mystical phenomenon with no apparent practicality. Many suggest that the concept of monogamy is too complex to understand. However, it's quite simple. Monogamy can be broken into two separate words: mono and gamy. Mono simply means one. Gamy means union. So, monogamy is defined as a harmonious agreement between two individuals uniting to become one. When two individuals truly become one (matrimony), a threefold covenant is established between God and the two partners.

In biblical days, anytime a covenant was established, there was a cutting of flesh and shedding of blood. A cutting tool would be used to sacrifice an animal. That animal would then be split in half and placed opposite of each person. The candidates for covenant would then walk through the path of the animal blood establishing the life-long covenant.

Marriage is no different. A similar covenant is established between a man and a woman. A man's penis represents the cutting tool. A woman's vagina represents the object being cut. When a man cuts into a woman's vagina, there is a shedding of blood, thus an establishment of a life-long covenant. Sex is more than just a physical act. It is a spiritual union between two individuals. Therefore, saying, "I Do" at the alter does not complete the union. Weddings are a public display before man and God of two people's commitment to one another. It is not until the sexual union takes place, that a marriage is consummated. This is why God's intention for sex was only for those within the confines of a marriage.

Too many people have spent their lives cutting, or being cut into, by people who weren't deserving of it. No life-long commitment was ever made. Marriage is for a lifetime. That is why vows conclude with the words, "Till Death Do Us Part." Meaning, the marital covenant can only be broken by death. It is a covenant that represents mental, physical and spiritual exclusivity. Anytime a partner seeks to satisfy a mental, physical or spiritual need outside of the covenant, infidelity is birthed and a breach of the covenant occurs. So, if a covenant can only be broken by death and someone willingly breaks the covenant, then the punishment for one's action could be death. Romans 6:23 says, *"For the wages of sin is death."* The death that one may face has many manifestations, including a relational, spiritual or physical manifestation.

Adultery can definitely cause a relationship to die. Some couples have successfully endured and overcome the pain that goes along with infidelity. However, many relationships have crumbled, despite the apologies, heart-to-heart talks, and countless counseling sessions. Adultery can lead to a spiritual death. When you sin against God, you clog up your lifeline with the Creator. Continual sin causes spiritual suffocation, ultimately resulting in spiritual death. Finally, adultery can lead to physical death. Several people have been killed (murdered) in the heat of passion. The rage of a partner has tragically caused many to take the life of another. These tragic endings may be far and few between, but they are realities. Proverbs 6:32-35 says, *"Adultery is a brainless act, soul-destroying, self-destructive; Expect a bloody nose, a black eye, and a reputation ruined for good. For jealously detonates rage in a cheated husband; wild for revenge, he won't make allowances. Nothing you say or pay will make it all right; neither bribes nor reason will satisfy him (TMB)."*

There was a time in history when people were flogged, stoned to death or run out of town if accused of adultery. Fortunately, these disciplines are no longer utilized. But there are punishments for adulterers today. About half the states in the U.S. retain laws against adultery that, although they are rarely enforced, would deny married persons who have extra-marital sex the right to vote, serve alcohol, adopt children, or raise their own children *(Constitutional Barriers, 1992).* Enforcing this legislation would really make people reconsider the next time they feel the urge to cheat.

Choosing Monogamy

For those of you who are struggling with monogamy or even contemplating the possibility of cheating, you must come to grips with the desire. By clearly determining your reasons for cheating, you may ultimately discover methods to a more fulfilling, monogamous relationship. So, how does one successfully embrace monogamy in a world that cries out for sexual promiscuity? It's simple. The bible is very clear on what our position should be. Romans 12:2 says: *"Don't copy the behavior and customs of this world, but be a new and different person with a fresh newness in all you do and think. Then you will learn from your own experience how his ways will really satisfy you (TLB)."*

It is pretty apparent that the multitudes of this world have traveled down a path of adultery and sexual immorality. However, we are not to walk down that same road. We are to be governed by a higher law. It is a law of integrity, discipline and order. In a world full of darkness, we have to be willing to uphold the torch of righteousness. The kind of righteousness that says, "My body belongs to God and God alone. I will not fornicate and live a promiscuous life. I will not destroy the sanctity of my marriage by committing adultery." But, how is this accomplished? Galatians 5:16,17 says, *"Walk in the Spirit, and ye shall not fulfill the lust of the flesh. For the flesh lusteth against the Spirit, and the Spirit against the flesh: and these are contrary the one to the other: so that ye cannot do the things that ye would (KJV)."*

It is important to understand that the spirit and flesh of a man operate according to two different laws. God governs the spirit and the flesh is governed by its own lustful desires. Whichever aspect of man controls the human system determines whether one walks down the path of promiscuity, infidelity, abstinence or monogamy.

God made man a spiritual being housed in a physical body. The spirit was designed to govern the human system. When the spirit leads the system it has an instant connection to the Holy Spirit and operates in a holy way. God explains the purpose for the indwelling spirit of man. Ezekiel 36:27 says, *"And I will put my Spirit within you so that you will obey my laws and do whatever I command (TLB)."* Well, what has God commanded singles to do? He constantly reminds singles to abstain from fornication (1Th. 4:3). Flee youthful lusts (2 Ti. 2:22). It is good for a man not to touch a woman (I Cor. 7:1). Do not be unequally yoked with an unbeliever (2 Co. 6:14). Discipline your body (Col. 3:5). Walk in the spirit so you will not fulfill the lusts of the flesh (Gal. 5:16). Married couples are given special instructions as well. You must not commit adultery (Ex. 20:14). Job, a married man, made a covenant with his eyes not to look with lust upon a girl (Job 31:1). Married couples are to do the same. Keep from the flattery of the tongue of a strange woman. Lust not after her beauty in thine heart; neither let her take you with her eyelids (Prov. 6:24,25). You must not be envious of your neighbor's house, or want to sleep with his wife (Ex. 20:17). Don't delight yourself with a loose woman or embrace the bosom of a stranger (Prov. 5:20).

Though the scriptures on marriage are written to a man concerning his dealings with a woman. The same principles apply to married women as well. These are very specific commandments that will keep you from falling into the sexual pit of self-destruction. Walking in the spirit of God is walking in the word of God. Though temptation may come, it will not lead to sin because your life is guided by God's commandments.

When the flesh is in control of the system it operates by what it can see, touch, taste, sense and feel. It will move the body to do things that satisfy the flesh. Well, what satisfies the flesh? Abstinence does not satisfy the flesh, promiscuity does. Monogamy does not satisfy the flesh, infidelity does. The very thing that God forbids usually satisfies the flesh of a man or woman. So, when someone commits adultery within a marriage, it is a direct result of the flesh in command. Regardless of the countless reasons men and women give for infidelity, they all point to the same thing: the flesh. The flesh says, "If it feels good, do it." The flesh says, "I know sex before marriage is wrong, but I can't wait." The flesh also says, "I know I'm married, but I can't deny my body the pleasure of another man or woman. The Apostle Paul wrote in Romans 7:18, *"For I know that nothing good dwells within me, that is, in my flesh. I can will what is right, but I cannot perform it. [I have the intention and urge to do what is right, but no power to carry it out](AMP)."*

Unfortunately, there is a battle going on within the heart of every man and woman as to which aspect will control the system.

110

Will it be the spirit or the flesh? The Bible explains this ongoing struggle in clear and simple terms:

"No matter which way I turn I can't make myself do right. I want to but I can't. When I want to do good, I don't; and when I try not to do wrong, I do it anyway. Now if I am doing what I don't want to, it is plain where the trouble is: sin still has me in its evil grasp. It seems to be a fact of life when I want to do what is right, I inevitably do what is wrong. I love to do God's will so far as my new nature is concerned; but there is something else deep within me, in my lower nature, that is at war with my mind and wins the fight and makes me a slave to the sin that is still within me. In my mind I want to be God's willing servant but instead I find myself still enslaved to sin. So you see how it is: my new life tells me to do right, but the old nature that is still inside me loves to sin. Oh, what a terrible predicament I'm in! Who will free me from my slavery to this deadly lower nature? Thank God! It has been done by Jesus Christ our Lord: He has set me free." Romans 8:18-25 (TLB)

The only way for singles to practice abstinence and married couples to practice monogamy is to make a committed decision to be led by the Spirit of God. You must allow your spirit, which is connected, to the Holy Spirit to run the human system. The only way to overcome your struggle is to feed your spirit and starve your flesh. There is a systematic approach to accomplishing this task:

1) Make A Committed Decision – In order to walk in the Spirit, a committed decision must be made. You must declare that the Word of God, both written and spoken, will become the final authority in your life. No matter how challenging times may get, you must make an uncompromising decision to obey the word of God.

2) Meditate On The Word – You must feed your spirit by meditating on the word of God. The Bible encourages everyone to meditate on it day and night. To meditate means to squeeze the nourishment and richness out of the Word and into your spirit. True meditation will cause you to respond to the Word with action. When you meditate on the Word it becomes easy to do. Therefore, obedience is a result of feeding your spirit with the Word. Disobedience is a result of an empty spirit. Psalms 1:2 says, *"But they delight in doing everything God wants them to, and day and night are always meditating on his laws and thinking about ways to follow him more closely (TLB)."*

3) Practice Spiritual Imagination – The words that you speak and the thoughts that you think produce images in your mind. So, whatever you are looking to produce in your life, you must get the image of that goal inside of you. If you want deliverance from sexual sin, get the image of sexual deliverance on the inside. If you want to live a monogamous life, get the image of monogamy on the inside. If you want to live an abstinent life, get the image of abstinence on the inside. Why is spiritual imagination so important? Simple. Imagination is the prerequisite for manifestation. Genesis 11:6 says, *"...and now nothing they have imagined they can do will be impossible for them (AMP)."* So, if you can see it, you can have it.

4) Subject Your Flesh Daily – Your body was designed to function as the temple, the very sanctuary, of the Holy Spirit. However, sin and the Holy Spirit cannot dwell in the same place. One must go. Your body does not belong to you, but to God. You are not your own. Romans 12:1 says you must *"present your bodies a living sacrifice, holy, acceptable unto God, which is your reasonable service (KJV)."* Before you start your day, your early morning prayer should be, "Father, I make you Lord and ruler over my flesh. Make my body obedient to what you want it to do. I bind the spirit of lust and declare it destroyed, right now, in the name of Jesus. I thank you for the victory over daily temptations. In Jesus' name I pray. Amen." This daily activity will ensure your spiritual success.

This four-step process will assist you in your pursuit of sexual morality. The daily execution of these steps will ensure that monogamy isn't just a way, but it's the only way.

Black Thighs
Black Guys
&
Bedroom Lies

The Game

Meeting In My Bedroom

School Days

Somebody's Sleeping In My Bed

Whatever Happened to Black Love?

Don't Wanna Be A Playa No More

Good Lovin'

Chapter Five

WHATEVER HAPPENED TO BLACK LOVE?

Conceived in a world of ethical, cultural and sexual perplexity, Wanda was vulnerably shaped by the iniquities of her progenitors. Trapped in the prisons of everyday life, this morally scathed soul soon became one flesh torn between two opposing worlds. One black, one white; One gay, one straight; one of sexual consent, one of rape, sodomy and molestation. A girl, whose innocence was robbed in an eternal moment, but was stolen over the course of time.

Wanda's body would no longer function in its normal adolescent capacity. It became victim to sexual dehumanization. Her eyes veiled the secrets of both a maternal homosexual indulgence and a paternal incestuous chase. Her mouth contained voiceless pleas for help. Her heart sustained the scorn earned by every hidden touch. Her womb forcibly embraced the unlawful entry of an adult male intruder.

Abandoned by her Black, heroin-addicted mother as a child, Wanda was forced to live with her white, sexually exploitive father and grandmother. The bible says, "Train up a child in the way he should go: and when he is old, he will not depart from it." Well, for eight years of Wanda's precious life, she was trained to use her body as a labor device for her father's lustful exploits. What started out, as a sporadic incestuous exchange soon became a frequent liaison. But no exchange was more memorable than the first.

It was approaching 1:30 am. Grandma Ester had already left for work, as she did every night at eleven o'clock. Daddy had just said goodnight to one of his married female friends whom he sexually entertained night after night. The house was now inhabited by a fearfully innocent daughter and a sexually opportunist father. Awakened by a disturbing dream, Wanda sought her father for consolation. Immediately receptive to her fear, he persuaded her to "sleep with daddy tonight." Without hesitation, she slipped between his sheets and into his arms seeking a comfort not often felt in the solitude of her own bed. However, within minutes her peace turned to panic as her father reached into her pajamas and began to fondle her in a way she had never felt before. Frozen in fear with no thought of what to do next, Wanda lied on the bed as her father continued to squeeze her body. After he penetrated her every crevice with his roving hands, he finally rolled over and fell asleep.

From that moment, every night became progressively worse. What started as just a touch, led to penal penetration and a ripped hymen. Wanda's sexual purity was stolen by the abnormal appetite of her own father. And for the next eight years, daddy's little girl would become his main obsession. While he entertained the pleasures of other women, the midnight hours were reserved for Wanda. Four nights a week over an eight-year period would equal the amount of times they indulged in sex. From the innocent age of four to the sexually precocious age of twelve, Wanda was forced to succumb to the perverted love of her father 1,664 times.

With no door to separate her room from the rest of the house, daddy would enter at any opportune time. While Wanda was sound asleep, he would slither between the sheets and into her bed. Awakened by the penetration of a thick finger slowly thrusting in and out of her vagina, Wanda knew "daddy has come." In her attempts to send him away she often played possum. Hoping he would leave, he continued to fondle her until she was forced to acknowledge his presence. With no words exchanged between the two, the look in her father's eyes said it all: "You know what to do."

Hesitantly, Wanda began to peel off her nightwear until she laid bare on her bed. With no recourse, Wanda's father began to climb on top of her almost physically mature frame. With Wanda hoping for a phone to ring or grandma Ester to return home early from work or a police raid to break up this heinous act, daddy continued to perform his dirty deed. Though Wanda was gripped and riddled with fear, she never denied her father because she felt she had no other choice but to comply. While subjugated as a sex slave within the dungeon of her own home, Wanda's mother Joan, now recovered from her addition, chose to come back into her life. Eager to find refuge in the presence of her almost forgotten mother, Wanda left her father hoping never to return.

Upon arriving at her mother's home, Wanda had soon come to learn of Joan's live-in roommate. Joan and Barbara had been friends for many years. The chemistry between them was second to none. There was warmth, love and understanding. However, they were more than mere roommates, they were lovers. It was a lifestyle that Joan never wanted her daughter to be exposed to, but felt that she was now old enough to understand. Now with Wanda's presence, they had finally become the family they always longed for.

Brought into a world of homosexuality after leaving a world of rape, sodomy and molestation resulted in Wanda's confused sexuality. Plagued with the thoughts of her father's relentless aggressions and astonished by the witnessing of two women making love, Wanda was emotionally distraught. This sensibility followed her even throughout her schooling. With both boys and girls acting as intrigued onlookers of her most alluring 36DD bust, her thick thighs and her protruding buttocks, at the tender age of fourteen, Wanda was confused about who she should become intimately involved. But Wanda ultimately made a decision. With an abnormal compulsion for boys due to her father's sexual conditioning, and an overwhelming curiosity for girls proposed by her mother, Wanda chose both.

Her first consensual sexual experience was with an eighteen-year-old girl. That peculiar encounter later developed into a yearlong relationship. Her name was Synclair. She was number one, then came Susan, then Robert. After him, Bryan, who was later followed by William, Latisha, and Jerome. Over the next few years, the list continued to grow. Larry, she met at the football game. Malik, she ran across at the bus stop. She met Nicole while walking home from school. Pretty soon, all they became were mere numbers, vague memories and obscure faces. Few developed into short-lived relationships, while most were merely one-night stands, midnight quickies, or long-awaited promises whose time had come.

Wanda's internal confusion and sexual compulsion drove her from one bed to the next, whether she was in a relationship or not. But, the bedroom experience did not just remain within the confines of a room. They extended well beyond the outskirts of her home. She indulged in sexual activity within hotels rooms, train stations, beachfronts, apartment rooftops, 25-cent peep shows, swimming pools, car seats, and city street corners behind high-rise buildings. In the midst of all the activity, Wanda wound up pregnant on three separate occasions. To no one's surprise, two out of three ended in abortion. The first termination occurred at the age of fourteen, and while most girls used their sixteenth birthday to celebrate life, Wanda used it to take a life. However, after her third pregnancy, at the age of twenty-four, she decided to keep the baby.

Though Wanda used sex as a way of getting back at her father, she often used it as a means to find true love or what she perceived to be love. However, every time she looked into the eyes of another man, all she could see was the reflection of her father. The pain, the hurt, and the torment of her childhood experience became too much for her to bear. While she once sought the arms of another man to heal her, they soon became the very things that drove her away. With well over one hundred men and several women now attached to her sexual past, the longing for a soft touch, a gentle embrace and a tranquil voice was never quenched.

Wanda believed that if she could please the men in her life with unrestrained amounts of sex and provocative attire, they would be more apt to stay. But every man kept coming up short. Wanda's failed attempt to find the love she sought permanently drove her to the other side. The emotional and physical connection that she so desperately yearned for was found in the bosom of another woman. Now living with her feminine lover, Wanda would expose Jason, her ten-year-old son, to the same homosexual proclivities that were exemplified by her mother.

Well, what happens next? Will Jason embrace an unnatural desire for men? Will he wind up like his perverted grandfather as a result of a generational curse passed down through the womb of his mother into the loins of his being? Or will he be haunted by the same sexual demons that drove Wanda down the path of promiscuity? One never knows.

And to think, it all started with just one touch. A touch carried out by a perverted father, a drunkened uncle, and a next-door neighbor; a touch smothered with a gross, insatiable desire for the forbidden. A touch that robbed her of the innocence of her childhood and exposed her to too much, too soon. A touch that has left her confined to the scrutiny of a counselor that cannot heal. All because of a single, solitary, sinister touch.

Unfortunately, the cycle continues to spin and many victims respond to their own vulnerabilities by becoming the villains that commit the same heinous acts. The cycle must stop now, for there is a severe punishment for those who perpetuate such a crime. Though no one has unveiled the coverings of their sinister ways, their deeds have not gone unnoticed. Their conduct may never be tried in the jurisdiction of this nation's court system, but they cannot get away. If they leave this earth faultless in the eyes of man, there is still another Judge they cannot escape. The Bible is very clear in its dealings with such individuals:

"But if you give them a hard time, bullying or taking advantage of their simple trust, you'll soon wish you hadn't. You'd be better off dropped in the middle of the lake with a millstone around your

neck. Doom to the world for giving these God-believing children a hard time! Hard times are inevitable, but you don't have to make it worse – and it's doomsday to you if you do." Matthew 18:6-7 (The Message Bible)

Wanda's circumstance is not uncommon. There are countless men and women whose sexuality has been victimized. Even as you turn the pages of this book, some adult brute with no moral conscience is inappropriately handling a little boy or girl. Many have never been made a statistic because, in order to be a statistic, they must tell. Many belong to the group that never talks or tells. Their childhood encounters remain a secret that's tucked away in the deep recesses of their minds.

It is a secret that follows that little boy and girl into adulthood, haunting them with the bitter memories of a distant past. While some have successfully dealt with their childhood drama, many more crumble to emotional pain, mental stress, disturbing dreams, and occasional reminders of people who possess the likeness of a past perpetrator. As a result, many adult men and women have become cold, callous, bitter, spiteful, vindictive, and non-trusting.

Based upon this harsh reality, the ultimate question becomes: "Can Black male/female relationships survive in America?" Not if chivalry has been replaced with a conniving endeavor to sexually exploit one another, and not if Black on Black love is dead. Well, is it really dead? Certainly not! For many, love has been dragged into a dark alley by a group of bloodthirsty scoundrels and beaten to a bloody pulp. Love has been precariously thrown into a dumpster and left to die. It's suffered severe stab wounds, crushed ribs, a collapsed kidney, and internal bleeding. Love's intestines have even been ripped out of its body and its eyeballs have been pulled out of its sockets. Now, lying on a cold hospital bed, in critical condition, Love is intravenously fed while oxygen is supplied by a life-support system.

Meanwhile, lust, bitterness and selfish ambition have taken center stage. The aforementioned bloodthirsty scoundrels represent the contributing influences that have sought to destroy Black love. These contributing influences consist of four things: one's family upbringing, past relationships, media and the hip-hop underworld of raw sexuality. Though there are countless factors that have negatively affected black male/female relationships, I will focus on these four.

Family Upbringing

As mentioned earlier, the Bible states, "Train up a child in the way he should go: and when he is old, he will not depart from it." Unfortunately, this principle stands true even in the worst state of affairs. Training is not limited to a strict or intense regimen of behavior to produce a result. It is often a conditioning process that one endures over an extensive period of time. The home becomes the nest from which most behaviors are shaped, and parents become the instructors from which most lessons are learned.

The relationship that a parent shares with a child is the most sacred of human relationships, apart from that of a husband and wife. The parent retains the greatest influence in a child's life. Even before birth, a child receives messages and emotions from the mother. The child within the womb can feel the treatment expressed from a father to a mother. For instance, if the father left the mother during the nine-month maturation period, the child could feel the depression, anxiety and abandonment experienced by the mother. In return, if the mother expresses hate for the actions of the father, the child absorbs the message of hate and anger. Therefore, everything a mother does, says, eats and feels affects the development of the child. Even after the child is conceived, the child's destiny will ultimately be shaped by what takes place in that household.

According to psychiatrists, psychologists, family therapists, and other mental health professionals, there is a great tendency to repeat a family pattern. This repitition is otherwise known as 'Indiscriminant Imitation'. It is when a child imitates any and everything that they see and experience in their environment. Most sexual problems stem from the deviations, failures or problems in the parent relationship.

Unfortunately, the Black family has suffered in part because of problems with parental relationships. According to a 2000 edition of the *Baltimore Sun*, approximately 66% of all African American marriages end in divorce. As a result, over ten million children under the age of eighteen have parents who are either divorced or separated. An August 1993 issue of *Newsweek* reported that a Black child has only a 20% chance of growing up with two parents until the age of sixteen. Due to these circumstances, single parents run almost 80% of all households.

The result of fatherless homes is devastating. Fatherless homes increase incidence of crime, lower educational attainment and add dramatically to the welfare roles. Beyond societal ramifications, fatherless homes have a devastating impact on male/female interpersonal relationships for both the mother and the child. "How?", you may ask. Let us analyze the following scenario.

Tosha grew up in a household similar to many others in her neighborhood. She was her mother's first-born child but her father's youngest daughter. Prior to meeting her mother, Tosha's daddy fathered six other children by three different women in the same neighborhood. But when Larry met Sharon, there was something about her he couldn't resist. She was undoubtedly the most physically attractive woman in the projects. After their initial meeting, they hit it off right away. Two months later, he moved in. Though never married, Tosha's parents lived together for five years. As the years added up, so did the tension in their relationship. Due to irreconcilable differences, Larry moved out. With a man no longer in the house, times got hard. Larry not only kept Sharon's bed warm at night, but he paid the bills. Sharon struggled raising a daughter alone. Left with no way out, she had to find a way to keep from getting evicted.

For the next thirteen years, Tosha grew up in a household where she saw her mother continually welcome a variety of men into her home. As a result, Tosha witnessed men offer gifts, provide money and have sex with her mother. When the rent was due, she slept with Leroy, the landlord. When the phone bill needed to be paid, she slept with Jim who worked for the phone company. When she needed groceries, she slept with Robert on the first floor. Sharon systematically provided for her household in this fashion month after month.

While struggling to raise one daughter, Sharon bore three more children by three different men. However, after being deserted for the fourth time, Sharon's attitude towards men completely changed. "Men ain't good for nothin'! All they want is sex and then run off." Sharon drilled this message into her three daughters and son. Though her attitude toward men changed, her behavior remained the same. And every new man Tosha and her siblings saw tiptoe out of the house was justified by the following statement: "The only one allowed to sin is this house is me. Do you understand?" Responding with a resounding yes, the children began to see through their mother's contradictions.

What child can endure such a lifestyle for most of his/her adolescent life and remain emotionally unscathed? How is it possible for a child to develop into a mature adult within these home environments? Many adults have employed a parenting style that ultimately pits males and females against one another. These unhealthy roles observed by both adolescent boys and girls give rise to adult men and women who remain at each other's throats, unable to fulfill each other's romantic expectations.

Dr. Larry E. Davis, author of *Black And Single* states, "Black women have become the men their mothers wanted them to marry." It suggests that Black women have been forced to become strong, highly independent protectors and the sole financial providers in the absence of men. Therefore, they have occupied the role of both mother and father. As a result, a female child is socialized to involuntarily act out a role that her mother was forced to play. Thus, the female child is embedded with a high masculine nature. Her masculine tendencies are brought into a relationship, leaving a man struggling with what role to play. It's challenging for a woman to know her role in a relationship if she's never had correct modelship. With the constant visitation of various men, girls are taught how to control, manipulate and deceive men with a power that rests between their legs.

Meanwhile, boys often witness a man who did not stay. His father, grandfather and uncle most likely didn't stay. So, commitment and staying power are never re-enforced. The absence of a male figure has left boys with little understanding of the emotional role they must play in a loving relationship. Generally, all they learn is what it takes to sexually attain a woman. While it's often said that food is the way to a man's heart, boys learn that money and gifts are ultimately the way to a woman's bedroom.

The dysfunction within the family unit has resulted in an ongoing emotional and sexual tug of war between men and women within the arena of love and passion. Unfortunately, this arrangement begins in the womb of a mother, and is perpetuated well into adulthood.

Past Relationships

Hurtful past relationships are one of the most destructive forces that stifle people's ability to love. Unfortunately, these relationships have a devastating affect on both a person's present, as well as, future well being. Often, issues leap out of the past and hold people hostage, forever chained to emotional pain. People who are still wrapped up in anger, bitterness and resentment suffer from a heart heavy with deep penetrating hatred. These are just some of the affects of a bad relationship.

A bad relationship is not the kind that goes through the usual periods of disagreement and disenchantment that are inevitable when two different people come together. A bad relationship is one that involves continual frustration, disappointment and undeniable hurt. They are full of verbal, emotional or physical abuse. Lies, deception and cheating become commonplace in many of these relationships. Such relationships destroy self-esteem and prevent those involved from moving on in their careers or personal lives. They are often fertile breeding grounds for loneliness, rage and despair. In bad relationships the two partner's lives are often on such different wavelengths that there is little common ground, little communication and little enjoyment of each other. Despite the pain, many rational and practical people find that they are unable to leave, even though they know the relationship is bad for them. One part of them desires an end, but a seemingly stronger part refuses or feels helpless to take any action. These relationships remind me of the biblical story of Lot's wife.

God was displeased with the relational lifestyles in the city of Sodom and Gomorrah and sought to destroy it. Because Lot had favor with God. He commissioned a group of angels to warn Lot and his family to leave the city and their lives will be spared. However, their only instruction was to flee and not look back. Unfortunately, as the family prepared to leave the city, Lot's wife looked back and instantly became a pillar of salt. She was destroyed because she disobeyed God and set her eyes upon the destruction of the city. Ultimately, the destruction of her past ultimately destroyed her.

Those like Lot's wife are guilty of looking back and revisiting the things in the past. As a result, they become salty. A sprinkle of salt is pleasurable, but a pillar of salt is disastrous. The deserts of the Middle East were landmasses of vegetation that were later destroyed by salt as a strategic act of war. So, while moderate amounts of salt are good for many things, large quantities are very destructive.

Salty people often see others through the same bruised and contorted eyes that they saw their past partner. This is a damaging behavior because wounds from the past can produce unwarranted suspicion, baseless comparisons, and fear of future intimacy. As a result, many wounded people build walls to protect themselves from the ill treatment of others. Their feelings and emotions are hidden behind cement walls. Those who purposely block out the pain, also block out potential pleasure as well. An emotionless person becomes an untouchable. Sermons don't touch them, hallmark cards don't touch them, flowers don't touch them and even a lover's warm and compassionate embrace fails to touch the unreachable place where their hurt resides. Their hearts are encased with ironclad plates protecting them from the pain and hurt imposed by others. Sadly, the protective walls and metal covering imprisons them in an intangible cell unseen by the eyes of others.

Joseph had been dating Clara for the last two years and, despite their small differences, the relationship seemed to be going pretty well. However, while Joseph sought quality time, Clara enjoyed the freedom of her space. Besides, she felt she had a life before she started dating Joseph and would continue to enjoy life well after him. Clara held companionship with two very special people. Other than her boyfriend Joseph, Clara's cousin Steven was very close to her. Clara and Steven spent lots of time together. He even spent weekends at the apartment while in town. Joseph soon found himself competing for time with Steven in the midst of his own relationship. This ordeal had carried on for seven months.

Naturally, Joseph became quite concerned and began snooping around Clara's apartment. One night, Joseph decided to show up unexpectedly and, to his surprise, Clara was rolling around in the bed with her cousin Steven. Immediately, a nauseous sensation began to arrest his body. His heart began palpitating at an alarming rate. Rage, disgust and hatred consumed his moderate 5'10" frame. It was at that critical moment that Joey realized that her cousin Steven was really Clara's secret lover for the past seven months. To no surprise, the relationship ended on that hideous night.

Joseph's mind was permanently stained and he involuntarily viewed all women through the same contorted eyes that he beheld Clara's dirty dead. Rather than allowing time for healing, Joseph immediately entered into another disheartening relationship. Joseph was a broken man looking for someone to save him and fill his void. He was seeking someone who would prove that she was not Clara. But he couldn't help living out his past in his present and his next girlfriend would ultimately become his victim.

Tammy was an honorable woman. Although, she had her share of male friends, she prided herself on commitment and loyalty. Joseph took a strong liking to her, but couldn't get past his issue of distrust. So, Tammy was forced to endure all of the insecurities that Joey bore in his past relationship.

He bought her a cell phone and pager to monitor her whereabouts. Tammy spent every lunch break at work on the phone with him as she ate her food to quell his insecurities. He monitored the amount of time it took her to get back and forth from work to ensure she was trustworthy. She was even instructed to disassociate herself with all of her male friends. And if there were ever a sign of incompliant behavior, Joseph would respond with the rage of a crazed man. Joseph's incessant behavior pushed Tammy over the edge. She decided that it was too much for her to handle. Within four months, the relationship was over.

Joseph allowed his insecurities from his relationship with Clara to pollute his relationship with Tammy. Sadly, Joseph is not alone. Many allow past hurts, pains, idiosyncrasies, inconsistencies, contradictions, faults and flaws to sift into new relationships. Not only do these issues stain an individual's heart and mind, but they often contaminate future relationships. Chris Jackson in his book, The *Black Christian Singles Guide to DATING AND SEXUALITY,* poses an interesting way of viewing past relationships. He states:

"Every modern airport is equipped with an electronic security device that scans carry-on items before we board our plane. The reason for the high-tech precautions is that in years past passengers began transporting unlawful materials or smuggling weapons that could endanger lives...Of course, it would not make much sense to check the passengers and bags after takeoff. Yet this is exactly what happens in many marriages and relationships. Many singles begin asking significant questions about their partners long after "taking off."...What if all singles were required to pass through a specially equipped and sensitive security check station before entering a new relationship?"

If people were required to go through a screening process before entering a new relationship, there would be far less mismatched couples. Many people usually enter into relationships unchecked. Many men often have a very shallow selection process, which generally focuses on the beauty of a woman. Likewise, several women have significantly lowered their standards just to find a man. With such superficial and incomprehensive means of selecting a partner, it is no surprise that relationships don't work. Long after the commitment to one another is made the facades and false faces begin to come down. Slowly, but surely, issues, secrets and insecurities begin to creep out. The toxic baggage of past relationships is gradually brought into present relationships. The trunk of unforgiveness and unresolved anger, the duffel bag of pain and repressed resentment, and the suitcase of possessiveness and dishonesty that has been piled up in the closet of one's life, severely tumbles into the lap of a lover once the hidden door is finally opened.

It is evident that the past can have a very nasty affect on both present and future relationships. So, how do we effectively deal with this problem? The Bible is very clear on how we should handle issues of the past. Philippians 3:13 says, *"No, dear brothers, I am still not all I should be but I am bringing all my energies to bear on this one thing: Forgetting the past and looking forward to what lies ahead, I strain to reach the end of the race and receive the prize for which God is calling us...(KJV)."*

There will always be pain and disappointment in life, especially within relationships. Therefore, one of the ways to effectively deal with the pain is to keep it where it is, in your past. Constantly dwelling on what has happened to you or what someone put you through will continue to make you a victim of your past. Learn to forgive yourself, as well as, the one who hurt you. Forgiveness releases the burden in your heart and makes way for the plans that God has in store for you. Yes, once you forget the things of your past and look forward to what is ahead, God will meet you where you're at and elevate you. Jeremiah 29:11says, *"For I know the plans I have for you, says the Lord. They are plans for good and not for evil, to give you a future and a hope (TLB)."*

I wonder what would've happened to Lot's wife had she never looked back. Where would she be? What would she be doing? I am certain that she would have enjoyed the relationships formerly established with her family. Learn from Lot's wife and look only toward your future so that love can once again inhabit your mind, body and soul.

Media

While many imitate what they see on television, hear on the radio, and read in magazines, these media outlets seek to reflect what is trendy or popular in society. Unfortunately, what is considered popular is often the worse that life has to offer. Materialism, immoral conduct and raw sexuality are among some of those favorite themes. This type of cat and mouse chase successfully perpetuates a skewed and sensationalized sketch of society. A constant diet of unhealthy words and images can have a damaging impact on positive and progressive relationships.

Media plagues many Black men and women with stereotypes and myths about black sexuality. Ironically, while many Blacks say that they detest these inaccurate images, they unconsciously personify them. One of the major reasons why relationships fail is because of the superficial standards used to determine a good partner. The relentless search for the highly-sexed, large breasted beauty and the financially and physically endowed stud excessively depicted in videos, magazines and romance novels leave many with shattered dreams and little hope for a brighter future.

One of the major contributors of this perpetual cycle is pornography. It gained its legitimacy in America when the sight of bare breasts in movies no longer raised protests or created goose bumps. Pornography has done a great job of distorting reality and setting people up for disappointment. There was a time when pornographers airbrushed nude women in magazines. However, with computer technology, women can be made to look drop dead gorgeous and physically perfect with computer enhancement techniques. This borderline artistic genre is built on pure deception because it turns women into something that they are generally not and leaves men totally oblivious to reality. Besides, centerfolds don't focus on the emotional and spiritual side of a person. They focus on genitalia, which can't fully satisfy any man's needs.

Most news stands stack magazines that are full of erotic content. Publications like *Cosmopolitan* and *Vogue* are seemingly obsessed with exploiting and influencing its reader's sex life. Publishers seek to seduce potential readers with sexually provocative sub-topics that glare at them from newsstand racks. These hook-line and sinker article topics include: Make him your love slave, 1500 confessions – What real women will and won't do in the dark, His and her pleasure triggers, 50 tricks for outstanding orgasms, Solo sex – he does it, do you? and 21st century sex dos and don'ts = ultra orgasms, love positions, and lust advice.com. With literary sexual themes reverberated in one issue after another, it is no wonder that this nation possesses such a gluttonous appetite for sex. The perversion doesn't stop there.

Late-night television remains bombarded with phone sex advertisements. A half-dressed Hottie will tantalize a man until he picks up the phone and places the call. Her only job is to bring that man to orgasm in record time. While most women in adult entertainment work hard to make men think they love sex and are attracted to all men, many openly admit that they hate men. Meanwhile, men hang up wishing their women were more like their phone fantasy. It has nothing to do with love and everything to do with lust. Therefore, it can never satisfy and always leave its followers wanting something that they, most often, will never have—perfection.

Mid-day soap operas such as *The Young and The Restless, As the World Turns, General Hospital,* and *Days* of *Our Lives* are like visual romance novels. Fans religiously tune in to watch these surrealistic television series that depict step-by-step enactments of infidelity, overbearing promiscuity, excessive greed, and scores of lies and deception. For many, they have become the how-tos of relationship immorality.

Talk shows draw heavily on relationship topics centering on family issues, sexual activity and dating. This type of content is abundant during morning and daytime hours when children have their greatest access to television. Talk-show hosts such as Ricki Lake, Jenny Jones, Montel Williams, Jerry Springer and Sally Jessy Raphael have all covered very rancid topics. The discussions normally include abuse, addiction, criminal acts, dating, mental health, parenting, physical appearance, racism, sexism, sexual activity, sexual infidelity, and sexual orientation.

Episode guests included: a mother who ran off with her daughter's fiancée; a man who appeared on stage with roses for the daughter he had sexually molested, and revealed that he had been molested when he was five; a 16 year old (wearing sunglasses to disguise her identity) who said she buried her newborn baby alive in her backyard; a pregnant women who boasted of having eight sexual partners during her first two trimesters; a woman serving as a maid of honor to her friend who alleged that she had slept with the groom a week before the wedding; and women who marry their rapists.

Young people exceed the number of adults who watch most of the morning, day, and nighttime programming that is aired. With all that is shown on television, it has been reported that young adults witness more than 15,000 sexual jokes, innuendoes and other references on television a year. Few, if any, deal with self-control, birth control, abstinence, and risk of STDs, pregnancy and HIV. In addition, according to Roger's *Silent War*, over 20,000 commercials annually viewed by young adults send across an implicit message that sex is fun, sex is sexy and everyone out there is having sex but you.

According to Henry Roger's *Silent War*, the three major networks: CBS, NBC, and ABC, broadcasted 65,000 references to sexual behavior in one year. That's 27 references per hour. Greg Lewis, author of the book *Telegarbage*, reported that references to intercourse on television, whether verbally insinuated or contextually implied, occurred between unmarried partners five times as often as married couples. With such a daily intake, it's no surprise that young people embrace lust over love, immediate gratification over commitment and promiscuity over celibacy.

So, who's responsible for producing such sordid shows? According to Roger's *Silent War*, a study was done in the mid-1980s of 104 of the most influential professionals in the television industry when things weren't quite as bad as they are today. The findings concluded that ninety-three percent seldom or never attend worship services. Ninety-seven percent believe pregnant women have the right to decide on abortion. Only five percent strongly believe homosexuality is wrong. Sixteen percent strongly believe that adultery is wrong. With beliefs like this, it's no wonder programming morally declined.

Sadly, this moral decline has penetrated its way into the hearts and minds of people across this nation. While most tout that the entertainment business has no affect on their relationships, they continue to suffer from divorce, loneliness, bitterness.

The Hip-Hop Underworld Of Raw Sexuality

If you take away Hip-Hop, you'd take away the voice of a generation of black youth and young adults. It's been one of the only venues where youth can verbally flex and truly be themselves. Hip-hop is a genre of music seen as a cultural vehicle for self-expression and social reflection of the community.

Birthed from the streets of the South Bronx, Hip-hop was originally used as a platform to educate and empower the nation on the realities of social and political Black America. Groups like Public Enemy, Brand Nubians, KRS-ONE, Tribe Called Quest, Queen Latifah, Arrested Development, and Poor Righteous Teachers penned lyrics that detailed and responded to the political agendas brewing in their community like police brutality, the prison system, Black on Black crime and drug infiltration. Today artists like Lauryn Hill, Common, Goodie Mob, Outkast, The Roots, Dead Prez and Mos Def have followed in that same tradition.

Unlike the early days, currently there is a war of the soul going on within the hip-hop nation. An overwhelmingly large segment of hip-hop music has transformed into a sample-heavy, highly materialistic, in-your-face-sexuality, cultural phenomenon that is far removed from its earlier social/political activism. Mass distributed hip-hop is now materialistic, hedonistic, misogynistic, shallow and violent. It boasts about a fantasy world of Versace clothes, platinum and ice jewelry, Bentley coups, Cristal champagne, crisp hundred-dollar bills, and unrestrained sex with no moral responsibility. The attitude toward male and female relationships in much of the music is strictly one of sexual supply and demand. Rap and R&B videos often expose more flesh than one is prone to see at the Freaknik. Many brothers stay home all day to watch videos and lust at every 'Video Hottie' that comes on the screen. This degenerate hip-hop message has seeped into the souls of both Black young adults and children stripping them of their moral core.

Most of the music selectively played on the radio highlights what is wrong with our relationships today: materialism, false definitions of man/womanhood, fornication, infidelity, homosexuality, and certainly the elusiveness of spirituality. So the ultimate question becomes, "Can Black male/female relationships survive in America?" A wise man once responded "Not if our young men continue to refer to young women as b---hes or our young women refer to young men as dogs or all of us refer to each other as niggers." These three disparaging labels have saturated hip-hop music like an uncontrollable virus. If you're in the hip-hop game it's likely that you are considered a nigger, which strips you of any cultural significance and leaves you morally bankrupt. If you're a man in hip-hop, you are depicted as a heartless, sexually indulged male brute (dog) who will sex anything with a pulse and even partake in another man's fruit. If you're a woman in hip-hop, you are depicted as either a hard b---h who will kill for her man, a fly b---h who can sex up her man, or a lesbian. So, there is no fullness of manhood or womanhood within the realms of mass-marketed hip-hop.

Male rappers have embraced the dog stigma of being a well-hung, heartless, sex-machine who can thrill any woman with his strong virile moves. They are also commonly referred to as 'Playas' and 'Ballers' which connote the same irresponsible behavior. This behavior is expressed through the music. Flip through an urban radio station and you'll hear the same ten to twelve songs all day long. By the time you recognize the song, you've heard talk of five sex acts, a gang rape and killing a girl who gets out of line. "What else can you rap about but money, sex, murder or pimping?" says Queens, N.Y.-based Ja Rule. " There isn't a whole lot else going on in our world." Dr. Dre said he tried to change directions in 1997, with his *Aftermath* album: "I have kids and wanted to get away from the 'b---hes and hoes and the violence, but I had to come back to the real. Back to the gangsta."

Many artists have responded, 'Rapping about it and doing it are two different things." Unfortunately, these so-called entertaining messages and images have shaped young people's behavior. With B.G.'s Cash Money colleague Baby, owning $100,000 worth of platinum dentistry in his mouth and Puff Daddy's high-rolling materialistic image, The Jewelers of American Emporium reported a 40% increase in the sales of white gold and platinum. With an overly saturated call to 'show your thong', Sisquo has convinced every female fan to run to the mall to purchase her own private collection of Vicky thongs. Certainly, if fans follow the latest fashion trends of hip-hop artists, their sexual attitudes toward women can be no different. With Juvenile touting 'Back That Azz Up' while rubbing his crotch and licking his lips, it's no wonder that brothers clock every female dressed in a flimsy halter top and tight skirt.

A classic example of the hip-hop dichotomy turned sour, is a comparative analysis between Erykah Badu and Biggie Smalls. On Erykah's second album *Erykah Badu Live*, she breaks down the significance of the Ankh. Erykah states that the Ankh can be broken down in three different parts. The circular or round part of the Ankh represents the womb of a woman. She then commissions the women to put their hands on their wombs. She then states that the elongated part of the Ankh represents the male principle of the birth canal. She then encourages the men to put their hands on their male principle. Erykah finally states, that the cross part of the Ankh represents the fallopian tubes. Therefore, each part represents 120 degrees of a larger 360-degree completion of life. Therefore, the unification of all three parts of the Ankh produces life.

In contrast, Biggie Smalls song, *The Players Anthem*, says the same thing in another way. He postulates, "Niggers grab your d—ks if you love hip-hop. B---hes grab your t-ts if you love Big Pop!" It is precisely the same thing being said in a sick, perverse way. While Erykah told the women to grab their wombs, Biggie told the B---hes to grab their t-ts. While Erykah told the men to grab their male principle, Biggie told the Niggers to grab their d—

ks. She used the Ankh as her cultural symbol and he used hip-hop as his cultural symbol. Can you see the difference? Erikah's descriptions of sexual organs were used for the purpose of procreation. Whereas, Biggie's descriptions of sexual organs were used as a form of self-stimulation to profess allegiance to a particular thing. So, many artists have taken the low road by expressing subject matter in a raunchy way.

Marriage doesn't even seem to maintain the same sanctity in the hip-hop game when you have Eminem rapping about cutting his wife's throat and locking her in the trunk of a car. DMX adamantly prides his wife, in an interview, on being a trooper for enduring his infidelity, which is exemplified in his video "What Them B---hes Want From Me?" Ice-T, also married, still professes to be a real life pimp, exploiting the sexuality of other women. L.L. Cool J, also known as the 'Guru of Pleasure' almost destroyed his marriage due to drugs and infidelity. However, he still features a different woman in his passionate surrealistic videos while assuring his wife and kids that it's all entertainment. Even Snoop Dogg allows his wife and three kids to rap along with his music as he refers to women as b---hes and hoes. The following are lyrics to songs that reinforce the dog stigma and relate to women in a dehumanizing manner.

I said I never saw a face like yours before,
And I been around some cute whores before,
That either me or my boys tore it up before,
So I'm hoping you different.
Let you push the six, and give you a different life,
And baby, if it's right,
Jump on it in the morning and ride it till the night.
Jay Z   'I Know What Girls Like'

Every time that I'm alone with you,
Homey be checkin' up on you,
But if that nigga only knew,

135

You gotta a lot of freak in you baby

Now every little thing that we do,
Should be between me and you,
The secret things that we do,
Let's keep it between me and you baby
        Ja Rule 'Between Me And You'

I get at these chickens from a distance
I start to stealin' the quickness.
The instance, they start catchin' feelings,
Then I'm out just like a thief in the night,
I sink my teeth in to bit, You thinkin' life?
I'm thinkin' more like what's up tonight.
Comon' ma', you know I got a wife.
Even though that p#$$y is tight, I ain't gonna jeopardize my life
What they really want from a nigga?
Somebody let me know!
        DMX   'What You Want'

     These lyrics demonstrate the dog stigma that dehumanizes women. However, the lyrics often go a step further. The visual esthetics of their musical videos portray women as nothing but eye candy. Hundreds of girls hustle to get the next coveted 'Video Hottie' spot. Video sets are filled with toned legs, flawless skin, extra-long weaves and curvy hips. While there may be legitimate models on the set, most girls make their living as nightclub dancers. Most Hottie veterans demand $1,000 day-rates and all expense paid travel, while keeping everything strictly professional. But a lot of girls perform sexual services behind the scenes to get those spotlight roles. Some feel they need to sleep with directors and artists to secure a spot.

     Meanwhile, many women have entered the rap game and accepted the b---h stigma: a sexually hot and bothered, ill tempered, malicious female. In the March 1997 issue of *Essence*,

Joan Morgan wrote, "The Bad Girls of Hip-Hop," and stated that "sex has become the bartering chips many women use to gain protection, wealth, and power." Entering an industry where millions have been made by pimpin' poontang, many female rappers have sold out for money by embracing the sex-me message. Rather than hip-hop being used as a vehicle to empower, several female artists have written artificial rhymes that welcome 'hittin' the jackpot between their legs.' This sexualized style of rap gets progressively worse because artists discover that in order to titillate a sexually overindulged society they have to be a bit more bold and edgy than the last artist. What they haven't grasped is that being sexy doesn't mean being nasty.

With an art form that continues to maintain a strong male presence, many female rappers have taken on the 'Bitch' stigma to sell albums. With a message that portrays a lifestyle of sex, drugs, money and rough street life, artists like Rah Digga, Mia X, Sole, Mocha, Trina, Eve and Da Brat have conveyed a message that has been deemed a total disgrace to Black womanhood.

However, no one has proven to be more sexually outrageous than hip-hop's nasty girls Lil' Kim and Foxy Brown. They have both exuded the ghetto glamgirl image, spewing raunchy pornographic and materialistic lyrics. Flaunting her blonde hair, blue eyes and silicone breasts, some hip-hop fans have argued that Lil' Kim has gone from rap queen to drag queen. Similarly, it has been said when Foxy Brown takes off all her make-up she looks like Doo-Doo Brown.

Rivaling for the number one Diva Ho spot, both Lil' Kim and Foxy Brown compete with one another to see who will take off the most clothing without showing every nook and cranny. While Foxy poses for *Vibe* magazine's cover grabbing her breasts and crotch, Lil' Kim attempts to top her efforts by wearing nothing but a hat and boots in a photo shoot for her second album. Lil' Kim declares "Sex is power; b---hes do what they have to do to get paid." In the same breath she states "I represent all the females." This is truly problematic. Meanwhile the Source stated that Foxy's second album "Chyna Doll is important because it provides a roadmap through the mind of a Black girl..." This is truly a scary statement. With very explicit messages that saturate radio airwaves across the nation, many have argued that these two artists have transformed more and more young female listeners into nymphomaniac, fowl mouthed, ill-tempered, malicious little girls.

Foxy Brown admits in the February edition of Rap Pages: "I'm not a role model, as far as what I say on my records. I say things that a role model just should not say. My fans just see Foxy and how it is our there. But that's not me. Foxy is just a character I become when I am out. At home I'm not like this at all. I am in my sweats and I am just chilling." Unfortunately, her admittance to a sex gimmick for mere entertainment is not enough. Foxy Brown's Pam Grier blaxploitation fantasy has ruined countless lives. Too many young Black girls have already had their innocence taken, their minds shattered and their lives destroyed. The following are lyrics recited by various hip-hop artists.

"I'm the baddest b---h, you gotta admit that,
69 ways, you know I'm wit that,
And I'mma shake my money maker,
I'mma shake this thing like a salt shaker,
Cause ain't nothin' wrong wit the bump and grind,
When I boot this thing up jump behind,
I ride like a choo choo train,
Little lim, I'm fittin' to do this thing.
Front, back, side to side,
That's how you slip and slide
What's little daddy, trick a fat stack
Representin' for my girls wit a fat back."
        Trina   'Pull Over, That A#$ Too Fast'

What would you do if your son was at home,
cryin' all alone on the bedroom floor cause he's hungry?
And the only way to feed him is to sleep
with a man for a little bit of money,
and his daddy's gone; somewhere smokin' rock now,

in and out of lock down,
I ain't got a job now. So for you, this is just a good time,
but for me this is what I call life.
      City High 'What Would You Do?'

Nuttin' make a woman feel betta than Berrettas and Amarettas,
butta leathers and mad cheddaz.
Chillin in a Benz with my ami-gos,
Tryin to stick a nigga for his pe-sos.
If you say so's, then I'm the same chick that you wanna get with,
lick up in my twat.
Gotta hit the spot,
If not don't test the poom poom nanny nanny, donny, heyyy!!!
      Lil' Kim 'No Time'

Aint no nigga like the one I got,
sleeps around but he gives me a lot.
      Foxy Brown 'My Life'

What's discouraging is that many of these artists think their message is truly empowering. That somehow being sexually free and materialistic is a step in the right direction for Black women. While Lil' Kim prides herself as being a self-proclaimed feminist, she admits to charging men for the pooh-nanny while seeking loving relationships. Akissi Britton, *Essence's* research editor and hip-hop fan, challenges Lil' Kim with a thought provoking letter featured in the October 2000 edition of *Essence* magazine. Akissi writes:

"I'm having a problem when all these voices are being classified as empowering and feminist...Just because a voice is feminine doesn't mean it's feminist...Feminism is about embracing our power without

139

reducing it to what's between our legs. And this so-called p#ssy power that you portray, the literal or figurative use of what's between you legs to get the material things you want, completely defeats this. Besides biggin' up every female who slept her way to the top, it perpetuates the gold-diggin', highly sexualized, whorish image that Black women have been trying to kill since slavery...

For too many years we female fans who lived, breathed and died hip-hop and have had to grapple with this ugly contradiction: How can we love the music that only sees us as bitches and hoes? And now you've come on the scene calling yourself a queen bitch, professing in your lyrics that the ultimate way to "get yours" is to be a supreme bitch and make men pay for a taste. What are we telling young girls, that the only way they can escape abuse, neglect and hard living – all by-products of sexism – is to use their bodies? That's praising prostitution.

Business fact of the day: Sex sells. But understand this: so does your soul. Ask yourself if you really felt empowered when you did an ad for your first album with your legs spread wide wearing only a thong and a bra. Did you feel empowered wearing absolutely nothing but a hat and boots during the photo shoot for a promo poster for your second album, *The Notorious K.I.M.*? If that image wasn't so profitable would you have done it? Money doesn't change the feeling of exploitation, does it? It just allows you to dress it up in furs, diamonds and designer clothes."

Though this article pointed to the image and message of Lil' Kim, it can easily apply to many female artists in the rap game. Yet, there's another cultural phenomenon destroying the minds of many of the popular hip-hop listeners: the excessive use of the word nigger (nigga). The Totally Unofficial Rap Dictionary defines nigga as a cussword originally used by white people, but taken over by Black people as a name to show their pride. Q-Tip said that it is commonly used as a term of endearment. 2 Pac professed that 'Nigga' meant non-ignorant, getting goals accomplished. Whether you spell the word nigger or nigga, the word is still negative. It's had a negative connotation since its birth.

Nigger comes from the Portuguese word "Negro." In *The Name "Negro": Its Origins and Evil Use,* Richard B. Moore wrote, "The first use of the word 'Negro' as a noun or name in relation to African people is to be traced back to the period after

1441, when the Portuguese explorers went down the African Coast. By the 17ᵗʰ century, the use of the term "Negro" as synonymous with "slave" was common in the British colonies in America, and remained that way through the end of the Civil War. "Nigger" is a phonetic spelling of the white Southern pronunciation of "Negro," and probably came into written use at a time when white America's spelling rules were lax. Despite the spelling, the word was synonymous with the word "slave." Southern slave owners sought to justify themselves by arguing that the "niggers" were not capable of being anything but slaves."

So when you refer to yourself or someone else as a nigger, you are really calling them a slave. This heinous word is not a term of endearment. It is a word used to degrade and dehumanize. Every time the slave master would crack his whip on the backs of Blacks, he would spit on them and call them niggers. Today, many people use the word 'nigger' like they're getting paid for it.

Black people will never truly be liberated until we change our language. If Black men continue to refer to women as b—ches, and black women continue to refer to men as dogs, and both continue to refer to each other as niggers, male and female relationships will always hunger for the respect it deserves. We created none of these names. They were created for us. Yet, we've taken ownership of these words and embraced them as our own. The excessive use of such words is just as damaging to the recipient as they are to the user. Rather than destroying a behavior, it's perpetuated by the constant use of a demeaning word. These words contribute to the breakdown of black love in male/female relationships.

Family upbringing, past relationships, media and the hip-hop underworld of raw sexuality are just a few of many factors that have damaged the very existence of Black people. If Black Love is to rein, we must begin to take responsibility for our own lives. We must not allow the negative circumstances of our past and present to poison our future. Don't follow in the tradition of Lot's wife by dwelling on your hurtful past (family upbringing and past relationships). If you do, it will destroy you, as well as your future relationships. Your dealings with the media should be very careful. You must guard your eyes from negative images and programming. The Bible says, *"Abstain from all appearances of evil.*" If you don't, it will corrupt you. Likewise, be careful the next time that you listen to the radio or pop in a CD (mass distributed hip-hop). "It is pleasant to listen to wise words, but a fool's speech brings him to ruin" (Ecclesiastes 10:12). Simply put, the continuous influx of negative messages will decay your moral and spiritual core.

In no way is the exposure of such sexually twisted messages and images an indictment on all hip-hop music. The hip-hop nation has influenced much of the cultural trends that have swept across this nation and the world. So, hip-hop is a significant part of the world's cultural fabric. When truth is conveyed, it should be done responsibly. Rather than seeking to glorify horrific conditions, expose it and recite lyrics that propose a plan of action to overcome them. Fortunately, there are countless artists that have successfully done this. Artists such as Lauryn Hill, Eryka Badu, Common, Gospel Gangstaz, The Cross Movement, B.B. Jay, the incredible Prodigal Sonz, and several others. While we listen to positive and productive lyrics we should seek to embrace the mass distributed hip-hop artists with loving arms. Allow that love and positive aura to consume their hearts, minds and souls so that conscious and uplifting hip hop messages can begin to spread like a virus. As a result, the lyrics can be used to help foster and maintain male-female relationships.

Bedroom Lies

The taste of salt
From tears of pleasure turned to pain
Hands roaming free
Discovering what could only be
Yours and mine
Inside you...I feel me
Two joined to become one
Unrealistic expectations have my imagination
To believe
That...this...could...be...L-O-V-E
A language misunderstood
Words spoken
From the body expression our hips, lips and fingertips
As we lay in this moment
Connected by the intimate touch of emotions
Turned to a sexual high
We can't deny the temptation raging from within
But must we defy the scriptures
To sell our souls to stranger
After stranger
After stranger
Our lives are in danger
And now we've become
Black thighs, Black guys & Bedroom lies

By Ladi Di

Black Thighs
Black Guys
&
Bedroom Lies

The Game

Meeting In My Bedroom

School Days

Somebody's Sleeping In My Bed

Whatever Happened to Black Love?

Don't Wanna Be A Playa No More

Good Lovin'

Chapter Six

Don't Wanna Be A Playa No More

How many times have you given your body away in flesh connections for a cheap thrill, bragging rights, a Coach bag or a bite to eat? How many of you are weighed down with guilt, shame and regret because you've offered up your holy of holies to countless men or women who were undeserving of it? How many vague names? How many unfamiliar faces? How many of you are heavy with burdens, hiding sexual secrets and suffering behind false faces?

Yes, sex can be an exhilarating experience, however, it often leaves many broken with low self-esteem, shattered, distraught and dirty. Most of all, sex has left countless men and women tired: tired of all of the meaningless sex, the emotional merry-go-rounds, sexual games, and bedroom lies. The behavior has led so many down the road of emptiness. It is often a road of fantasy that offers no fulfillment or future. Many players are never seriously considered as potential partners because of their game-like ways and tactics. The players are often only seen and dealt with on a strictly sexual basis, rather than looked upon as viable candidates for long-term relationships.

Interestingly, many men and women want out of their sexship or relationships, but find it difficult to let go and call it quits. Though several Black male-female relationships are strangled by the weeds of selfishness, exploitation, deceit, and faulty expectations, breaking up or letting go is hard to do. As hard as it is to let go, it is essential for living a healthy and productive life. The problem is that masculinity and femininity have been firmly entrenched within the context of sexual relationships with members of the opposing sex. So, if a relationship or sexship is not established, it often leaves many with no identity or sense of self-worth. However, once true definitions of masculinity and femininity begin to surface in the minds of men and women, it will soon be discovered that the playa' persona is nothing but a trip down a dead-end road.

Playin' Is Played Out

Many people who participate in sexual games and bedroom lies often become the very victims of the games they play. Thus, left with no way to recover or redeem themselves. However, others have been blessed by God's grace to turn around and get themselves together. The very ones that should be lying up in a hospital bed or even buried six feet under have overcome what others have not been able to escape. God's mercy is truly great. There is still time to follow the decision of the prodigal son and come back home.

The following four accounts are individuals who represent prodigal sons and daughters who have made the choice to come back home. They have decided to give up their playa ways because playin' is just plain played out.

Sharonda 24, single

"I fell into a pattern of meaningless relationships. I found myself jumping in-and-out of different beds. Destined to find my prince charming, I experienced more hurt and pain than I did love and happiness. Like most women, I equated sex with love. Rendering my body for the sake of finding love was a plan that failed every time. I was at my breaking point. With a desperate cry I screamed NO MORE! My body was tired. My eyes were swollen from the tears that I cried night after night. My heart and soul ached with an unbearable pain. I was at my breaking point.

After ten years of physical and emotional pain, I wanted to heal. I no longer wanted to live a life of sexual sin. No longer having sex for the sake of sex. I no longer wanted to be involved in meaningless relationships. I made the decision to abstain from sexual intercourse. I became celibate. Free to focus on loving me and understanding my life's purpose. Now, my mind is free. My body is free. My spirit is free. I am enjoying my freedom. I no longer look for love. I realize that no matter how good a man looks, or how well he performs in bed or what he does for a living, it cannot give me true love. True love is God's love. The love I was searching for was with me all the time. It wasn't until I Let Go and Let God that I experienced the feeling of true love."

Franklin, 32, engaged

"I always loved women. I was raised to. Actually, I was raised to lust women. I had ten uncles and seven of them were pimps. All seven were married with children and had women on the side. They exposed me to the life of cheating, broken relationships and pimpin' at the tender age of 13. The more women I had, the more of a man I was considered. By the time I was 17 years old, I had three girls working for me. I sexed them. I protected them. I got them out of jail when they were arrested for prostituting. I was their father, their lover and their best friend. In all actuality, I was their god. But, that was not all. I've had sex with so many women that I've lost count. Skinny women, fat women, pretty women, ugly women, Black women, White women, Puerto Rican women, handicapped women, even women I hated.

I had no respect for them. I treated all women like cigarettes. A man smokes a cigarette when he's hungry, bored, mad or tired. Well, that's exactly how I sexed women. I've even raped a couple of women in my day. I never used condoms and would cum inside of every woman that I slept with. These women were consumed with spirits that ultimately jumped on me; suicide, depression, greed, loneliness and nymphomania. Most of my life I've had to battle with these spirits and always sought a way out. I wanted to change but my flesh kept pulling me back into the very thing that I wanted to get out of. I was sick and tired of falling into the bosom of another woman. So, I sought the Lord and asked Him to change me. It took years for me to finally purge myself of all of my past. But I am now truly delivered. Abstinence is the best thing that could have ever happened to me.

Felisha a.k.a. Bronze, 21, single

For the past two years I supported my way through school as an exotic dancer. While most brothers stood on corners selling drugs to survive, I stood on tabletops selling flesh to survive. I gained satisfaction by making men cum in their pants while performing lap dances. I touched men. I teased men. I detached men from their wallets for a quick peek at something they knew they could never have. I have even performed lesbian acts on stage for a few extra dollars at the end of the night. I often allowed men to fondle me for a quick buck. But with the brutish fondle of every foreign touch, my hatred for men began to intensify. I would purposely get drunk and high before a performance, so that I would remain oblivious to men's doggish chants and physical aggressions.

When money was tight, I subjected my body to back room sex sessions with customers who were willing to pay. But I was not alone. The clubs I worked for often had 'Lock-Ins' which were never announced. Clubs would lock all doors as if they were closed. Within minutes the strip club would turn into a whorehouse. Other dancers would have sex for money and weed. The floor was often carpeted with unwrapped, loosed and used condoms. The club always smelled like cuchie. I hated what I was doing but it was the only thing that could support my lifestyle. Well, towards the end of my second year as a dancer, I was raped and impregnated by a customer who had been watching me for the last 3 months. The humiliation, fright and despair drove me away from the business, never to return again. I was sick for weeks. I got an abortion and promised never to disrespect my body again. I cried out to God to forgive me, to heal me, to touch me. I desired a touch much different than what I had been used to. I wanted a touch that would heal the inner depths of my soul. Because of God's comforting embrace, I know longer seek the pleasurable touch of another man.

Aaron, 26, married

For six years I have struggled with the spirit of lust. I was never a real promiscuous man, but the desire for sex kept me trapped in a self-destructive behavior. Understanding that sex was off limits until marriage, I often settled for the next best thing, masturbation. It was an excessive, compulsive habit that often drove me to the point of no possible return. Masturbation was a drug my body craved for. I often compared myself to Pookie, in New Jack City, simply because the drug that I had eternally been addicted to kept calling me. Anything that remotely reminded me of the pleasures of sex, resulted in a self-stimulating one-man-show. Late-night movies, women magazines, sexually explicit music, porn music videos and large breasts drove my past temptation into the wiles of physical pleasure. Vaseline, lotion, naked pin-ups, private porn tapes and a vast imagination were the tools I used to meet my sexual high.

My dirty deed was not limited to a late-night visitation within the solitude of my own home. On the contrary, it accompanied me at all times, spaces and places. It followed me into public bathroom stales, street alleyways, behind parked cars, woodsy areas and even in grid-lock traffic. While people often left non-smoking public areas to inhale a soothing but fatal nicotine stick, I often left public premises to relieve a burning fire sparked from within. Though the pleasurable indulgence soothed the savage beast that lay within, it often caused me to drop to my knees in guilt, pity and shame. That's not all. My eyes, knees, and spine weakened which caused me tremendous physical harm. I cried out for help, but no force was strong enough to rescue me from my own deplorable pit of destruction. I tried almost everything but nothing seemed to work. But it wasn't until I emersed myself in the Word of God that changes began to take place. The scripture convicted me and gave me a step by step solution for finally overcoming a habit that could have ultimately destroyed my life. The scripture will never be able to kill the urge and craving that periodically seeks to consume my body, but it can stop the lascivious spirit in its path and declare it defeated in the name of Jesus.

Maybe your life story is more tragic than the aforementioned experiences. Maybe not. Whether you've taken on the practice of homosexuality, bisexuality, heterosexual promiscuity, or whether you've been with just one soul, there is still time to come back home. It is too important to put off another day. It is not a decision that you can afford to make next week, next month or next year. You've got to do this thing right here and right now. Choose celibacy for today so that you can truly live for tomorrow.

Struggle To Stay Pure

Making a decision to live a celibate life after you have undoubtedly enjoyed the pleasures of sexual gratification is not an easy task. Just because you've made a personal declaration to abstain from sex until marriage doesn't mean that the horniness and the erotic thoughts and memories of passionate nights will leave. There are going to be times when you feel extremely horny. There are going to be times when loneliness weights heavy on you like a ton of bricks. As a matter of fact, horniness and loneliness are two of the biggest obstacles individuals who practice celibacy face. Unfortunately, many men and women have thrown in the towel to avoid climbing into an empty bed for one-night-longer. They have suffered from penis and vagina withdrawal or the reality that no one else can be keep their beds warm at night.

Celebrity Jane Fonda once said, "I've never felt this kind of pain. It leaves you raw and vulnerable. Now when you're faced with something that painful, you have two choices. You can go down, go under – just cave in, out of fear of what it means to be single again. Or you can say this is to open a door that I've never even thought of opening." You've gotta ask yourself the question: "Do I really want to go through this all over again? Is being with someone, just for the sake of sex or companionship, worth all of the pain and agony that goes along with it?"

You may be one who says, "I can't control my sex drive" or "I just can't help it. When I'm alone with someone of the opposite sex that I'm attracted to, I can't help myself." But the behavior you say you can't help is performed by an act of the will. There is a conscious will to peel off your clothes, jump into bed and engage in sexual behavior. Your body cannot tell your mind what to do. On the contrary, your mind tells your body what to do. You may be one who says, "Everyone else is doing it, so why can't I? I'm missing out on what everyone else is doing and it's not fair." One thing that should be kept in mind is God's judgment on uncontrolled sexual behavior. Those who engage in such activity cannot enter into the kingdom of God. So, a few orgasms are not worth an eternity in darkness.

So, what can be done, once and for all, to break away from improper sexual activity? How do people handle their feelings and desires for sex? What should people do with all of their built up sexual energy screaming to come out. Unfortunately, some resort to alcohol and drug abuse, overeating, excessive masturbation, compulsive spending and unhealthy sexual affairs. But, there are some practical steps to overcoming promiscuity.

1) Make A Quality Decision

In order to truly conquer the sexual struggle to stay pure, the first step that must be made is a quality decision to end all sexual behavior. However, first you must acknowledge your behavior as sin. Unfortunately, many people don't talk about sins today; they talk about problems. The reason that problems are more convenient than sins is simply because people don't have to do anything about them. If you have a problem, you can get sympathy for it, understanding for it, and even professional help for it, to name a few. Sins, on the other hand, have to be repented of, confessed and forsaken. You can put away the sinful habits that have mastered you if you truly desire to do so. You must accept your personal responsibility for them. It is ultimately up to you to determine whether you're going to let your body be used for sin or for righteousness.

Without a quality decision being made, it's easy to be delivered from sexual sin just to find yourself right back into what you just got out of. It's important to understand that your death to sin has finally ended your relationship with sin as master, but it hasn't terminated its existence. Sin is still alive, strong, appealing, but its power and authority have been broken (Romans 8:2). Furthermore, your flesh did not die either. You will still have memories, habits, conditioned responses, and thought patterns ingrained in your mind that will prompt you to focus on your own sexual interests and desires. Though you are no longer in flesh, you can choose at any moment to walk according to your flesh, complying with those old urges to satisfy yourself instead of God.

The thrill of sexual calisthenics may never go away. The desire to be loved and feel romantic may always exist. No one promised the feelings to go away. But, regardless of what your body may cry for, the quality decision of abstinence must still be made. Simply put, promiscuity is never beneficial. It is not beneficial to have sex with someone, hoping that a commitment will follow. It is not beneficial to have sex with someone you barely know. It is not beneficial to use sex as a way to get to know someone. It is not beneficial to use sex to experience instant intimacy. It is not beneficial to use sex in an attempt to hold on to someone. It is not beneficial to engage in sexual relations with a person just because it feels good.

Promiscuity is a behavior that will often leave you torn, broken, emotionally drained, resentful, cynical, untrusting and spiritually depleted. Though, the physical act may possibly give a pleasurable experience, the ramifications of such activity makes the act not worth it. So, make a quality decision today to avoid the lust of your youth and choose celibacy.

2) Walk In The Spirit

As mentioned in earlier chapters, the only way to overcome lust and live a sexually pure life is to walk in the spirit. To walk in the spirit means to walk in the word of God. Psalms 119:9 asks,

"How can a young man cleanse his way? By taking heed according to Your word." It goes onto say in the eleventh verse, *"Your word I have hidden in my heart, that I might not sin against you."* God's word not only purifies us from sin, it also prevents a sinful behavior.

Romans 6:12,13 instructs us on how to relate to sin: *"Therefore, do not let sin reign in your mortal body that you should obey its lust, and do not go on presenting the members of your body to sin as instruments of unrighteousness; but present yourselves to God as those alive from the dead, and your members as instruments of righteousness to God."* Your old evil desires were nailed to the cross with him; that part of you that loves to sin was crushed and fatally wounded, so that your sin-loving body is no longer under sin's control, no longer needs to be a slave to sin; for when you are deadened to sin you are freed from all its allure and its power over you. Romans 6:6-7 (TLB).

Reading and meditating on the word of God day and night will cause your mind to be renewed. No longer will it be carnal in nature, but spiritual. Your mind will line up and agree with the laws of the book and obedience will ultimately follow. Make a habit of reading the word continuously so that you will be able to successfully walk in the spirit.

3) Guarding Your Gates

Are you guilty of living a secret thought life? Would you be embarrassed if others knew what went on inside your mind? Each of us leads a secret thought life, an invisible life known only to God and ourselves. For some of us, our secret thought life consists of a dream world of fantasies that concoct intricate plans that fulfill lustful desires. Others of us fabricate chance meetings with beautiful women or handsome men who seduce us. We each invent secret images of what we want, which we would be embarrassed for others to know. Unless we develop a solid understanding of how our thoughts, motives, and ambitions are shaped, we will have impure secret thoughts, wrong motives, and selfish ambitions. If we don't leave a gatekeeper posted at the gates that lead to our inner being, then the enemy can slip into our thoughts under the cover of low awareness.

II Corinthians says, *"We must take captive every thought to make it obedient to Christ* (NIV)." Why, you may ask? Ecclestiastes 12:14 says, *"For God will bring every deed into judgment, including every hidden thing (our secret thought life), whether it is good or evil* (NIV)." Our prayer should be the prayer of King David *"Search me, O God, and know my heart; test me and know my anxious thoughts. See if there is any offensive way in me, and lead me in the way everlasting* (Psalms 139:23,24)."

There is a very strategic way of controlling our thought life and purifying our minds. We must become gatekeepers. Each of us possesses gates that allow information to enter into our minds, whether positive or negative. These gates are the eye gate, ear gate and mouth gate. Once these gates are properly guarded, the struggle for sexual purity weakens significantly.

First, you must guard your eye gate. The Bible instructs us to avoid all appearances of evil. What does this mean? Well, anything that triggers our minds and bodies to desire sex should be avoided at all costs. Therefore, HBO and Showtime late-hour flicks, MTV and BET hip-hop and R&B porn videos, and Penthouse, Hustler, Playboy and Playgirl may not be the best way to entertain you. If your visual diet is consumed with beautiful faces, large breasts, soft and wet skin, protruding behinds, bulging groins, hard nipples, biceps, triceps, and rippled stomachs, it will unmistakably stimulate your mind and trigger bodily responses causing hard erections and moist appetites. Your eye gate should be consumed with the word of God. Your entertainment should be tasteful and full of moral content.

Second, you must guard your ear gate. The bible says that evil communication corrupts good manners. Therefore, you must be careful what is being communicated to you on a regular basis. Romantic R&B and sexually explicit hip-hop and rap lyrics should be avoided. Music has the potential of creating an atmosphere and mood that is conducive for sexual intimacy. Furthermore, you should guard your ears from stand-up comedy that is very sexual in nature. Conversing with others about their sexual experiences is also a very dangerous activity to engage in. Your ears should be consumed with the word of God, in the form of preaching, and spiritual music that seeks to edify your spirit rather than provoke your flesh.

Thirdly, you must guard your mouth gate. The Bible says from the issues of the heart, the mouth speaks. What this means is that whatever you feed the heart and mind of a man, will eventually come out of his mouth. Your conversation should be pure in nature. The Bible instructs that the word of God and Godly things should constantly be spoken from your mouth. Only that which is edifying should be spoken to yourself and others. By controlling all of these gates, your mind should be clear from sexual perversion, fantasy and memory.

Once you have successfully overcome the spirit of lust by living a celibate life, learn to enjoy the season of singleness.

The Season Of Singleness

To everything there is a season, and a time for every matter or purpose under heaven. Ecclesiastes 3:5-6 says there is *"a time to embrace and a time to refrain from embracing. A time to get and a time to lose, a time to keep and a time to cast away."* These scriptures can easily speak of one thing, the season of singleness. Singleness is a season that allows you the opportunity to seek the presence of your own personhood. It's a time to entertain yourself. It's a time to plan an extended amount of time with yourself to discover the thoughts, passions and dreams of your life.

Few people embrace this season for the blessing that it is. Rather, they loathe the state of singleness. Bedtime is probably the loneliest time of the day for singles, and it's when all the old issues scream for attention. Many equate the state of being alone with loneliness. But being alone doesn't necessarily mean that you are lonely. Loneliness is a sense of solitude filled with gloom and an unfulfilled yearning for companionship. Lonely people endure their time alone as if they have been exiled to solitary confinement.

Unfortunately, many people enter into relationships because they claim that they are lonely and need someone. Few realize that loneliness is not solved by sharing companionship with another person. Loneliness is caused by an emptiness that comes from within. It's a need for affirmation and confirmation. It's a need for someone to make us feel good about ourselves so that we can be assured that someone likes, cares and is attracted to us. It is a special need that cannot be met by another man or woman. It is a need that is not only shared by singles. Many who dwell within relationships also feel a since of loneliness. This need can only be met by establishing a relationship with God. Only He can touch the spot that no one else can reach.

Alone is where we start in life and essentially where we will end. Therefore, we should learn how to function in this world alone. Only then will we be able to seek from others the kind of love and affirmation that first comes from within. Silent time alone allows us to explore our commitment to our own well-being and fortitude. In order to be productive people, we must develop the ability to fully embrace ourselves in the solitude of our own existence.

In order to properly operate within the season of singleness, you must understand the difference between being separate and being single. To separate means to part, withdraw or terminate a relationship. You can decide to physically separate yourself from a person or relationship and not truly be single. As long as your thoughts, feelings, emotions, dreams, heart and mind are still with the one you have separated from, you are not yet single. There are many people who have ended relationships, but still maintain an emotional connection, whether good or bad. Even if you are holding resentment, rage and anger against a former lover, you have not yet entered into the season of singleness.

True singleness is something that everyone should strive for. It means that you are whole and complete within yourself. It means that you aren't lacking anything. When you are truly single you look for someone to complement you, not complete you. When you are truly single you are alone but never lonely, for alone means all one. The Bible speaks of having a 'singleness of mind' and a 'singleness of heart'. Simply put, your heart and mind should be on strengthening and developing yourself through the power of God.

I Corinthians 7:34-35 says, *"I want you to live as free of complications as possible. When you're unmarried, you're free to concentrate on simply pleasing the Master. Marriage involves you in all the nuts and bolts of domestic life and in wanting to please your spouse, leading to so many more demands on your attention. The time and energy that married people spend on caring for and nurturing each other, the unmarried can spend in becoming whole and holy instruments of God (The Message)."* Your season of singleness is truly a gift from God because it frees you up from dealing with the major responsibilities married couples deal with. It gives you time to heal from past relationships and reflect on mistakes made. The season of singleness is an unparalleled opportunity to grow spiritually, personally and financially.

1) Spiritually

There is no better time to develop your spiritual relationship with God than when you're single. You are not bombarded with all of the issues couples have to endure. It can be effectively used as a state of complete intimacy between you and God. A time to heal from your sexual past. A time to be completely purged of all of your sexual indiscretions. A time to surrender your life to a higher power, admitting that you are incompetent in handling your own affairs. A time to start over.

In order to successfully travel down the road of spiritual development, there are certain things that you must commit to do. First, you must sincerely forgive whoever may be responsible for your pain. One of the biggest obstacles to developing your spirituality is the inability to forgive. Second, you must accept God's forgiveness for your sexual past. Third, you must crown Jesus Christ Lord over your life.

So, someone hurt your feelings? Do you get angry whenever you hear their name mentioned? Have you made plotting revenge a favorite pastime? If so, you may be a victim – a captive of your inability to let go of the hurt caused by others and move on with your life. Fortunately, you don't have to remain angry. Your ability to forgive others is one of the most important tools on your road to spiritual and emotional recovery. When you extend forgiveness to wrongdoers, you are the ultimate beneficiary. Forgiveness, essentially, is the act of setting someone free from an obligation to you that is the result of their wrongdoing. It does not, however, result in that transgression being wiped from your memory. It can give hope and stimulate reconciliation. It recognizes and honestly handles the flaws, failures and fallibility that exist in every human being and in every relationship.

In order to heal from your past sexual sins, you must repent of your sins and ask God to forgive you. John 1:9 says, *"If we confess our sins, he is faithful and just and will forgive us our sins and purify us from all unrighteousness* (Isaiah 43:25)." *"I even I, am he who blots our your transgressions, for my own sake and remember your sins no more. Therefore, there is no condemnation for those who are in Christ Jesus* (Romans 8:1)." The key to this working is repentance. Repentance means to feel remorse or self-reproach for what one has done or failed to do and make a change for the better. Simply put, go and sin no more. Unfortunately, most people offer an apology and a declaration to never do a particular deed again. However, that doesn't work. There is no power in a declaration. Therefore, the sexual behavior is never broken. You can't willfully continue to engage in sexual activity and ask God for forgiveness. You've got to make a quality decision to break away from all sexual ties. Then and only then will the healing process begin.

Lastly, you must make Jesus Christ your personal savior and crown Him Lord over your life. Ephesians 2:1-3 describes our nature before we came to Christ: *"You were dead in your trespasses and sins, in which you formerly walked according to the course of this world, according to the prince of the power of the air...and were by nature children of wrath."* Our very nature was sin, and the result of our sin was death. However, through salvation God changed our very nature. We became *"partakers of the divine nature, having escaped the corruption that is in the world by lust"* (2 Peter 1:4). You are no longer in the flesh; you are in Christ. *"Therefore if any man is in Christ, he is a new creature"* (2 Corinthians 5:17).

God wants to get us alone to present ourselves holy before him. The root word holy means to be separated and set apart for God, consecrated and made over to Him.

2) Personally

Relationships can often be very distracting and cause individuals to totally forget about themselves. They take enormous amounts of time and energy. Couples often spend untold hours talking, thinking and worrying about their relationship, which often robs individuals from other pursuits. They have the capability of distracting people from developing their abilities, skill sets, visions and dreams. Relationships exhaust time both could have spent developing skills and exploring new opportunities. The truth is, most get involved in relationships and totally forget about their own self-improvement. We forget the day of the week. We are often oblivious to the things going on in the world.

However, singleness gives you all the uninterrupted time you need to focus on yourself and no one else. That's truly a gift. You can engage in strategic life planning. You can work on projects that were once delayed because of past relationships. You can work on personal self-enhancement. When focusing on your personal well being, there are some revolutionary questions that you should daily ask yourself. "Who am I? Am I all that I say that I am? Am I really all that I ought to be? What is the purpose for my life? What have I been sent here to do?" These questions give you time to think about your values, goals, and dreams. Time alone can be spent revisiting important areas of your life: emotional and physical health, education, career, and most important spirituality. Your season of singleness is an excellent time to chase your dreams and fulfill your most intimate desires in life.

In order to discover your true passions in life, engage in the following activity. Find a place where you can be alone and uninterrupted. Clear your mind of everything except what you are going to read. Just focus and open your mind. In your mind's eye, see yourself sitting down in a rocking chair surrounded by your grandchildren. Visualize their captivated faces filled with expressions of excitement as they gaze into your presence. Hear their murmurs of intrigue as they respond to your melodious voice, and feel the warm presence of your mortal inheritance.

As you sit there, you suddenly come face to face with yourself. Some of your grandchildren ask you to tell them all about you. They want to know about your family, community, spiritual and financial career/lifestyle. They want to know the essence of your success. Now think deeply. What would you like them to know about you? What character would you like to convey to them? What contributions, and what achievements would you want them to remember? Try to capture the essence of the lifestyle you want to have created through your day-by-day investment over a period of that many years.

The purpose of this exercise is to teach you the art of visualization. Visualization ultimately determines your destiny. Through the powers of imagination, you can visualize your own definition of success. The exercise will help you properly place your goals, dreams, objectives, and even your fantasies. Relax and let the ideas pour from both your conscious and subconscious. Don't evaluate your potential for achieving each item. Once completed, write out your own career path, determine what you want your income to be, and how you plan on utilizing your source of wealth. Actually write it out. Be specific.

_____

_____

_____

_____

_____

_____

_____

_____

_____

_____

_____

_____

Stephen Covey, author of *The 7 Habits Of Highly Effective People*, says to "begin with end in mind is to begin today with the image, picture, or paradigm of the end of your life as your frame of reference or criterion by which everything else is examined. By having a proper understanding of your end in mind, you can make certain that your day-to-day activities do not deviate at all from what you regard as important, and that each day of your life contributes to the vision that you have of your life." If you can clearly define what you want your grandchildren to know of your life…if you can clearly define what you want your grandchildren to know about you, you will find your definition of success.

We all obtain the ability to determine our destiny through the process of visualization. What you write will excite you, motivate you, inspire you, make you laugh, and most of all, define desires and dreams that all too often are ready to surface but are held back by the complexities of life. Once you have made your list with no limitations, choose those objectives which are most important to you. After you define your visions, the things you want to be and the things you want to accomplish, the next logical step is to build your roadmap.

3) Financially

One of the major issues in Black male/female relationships is money. It is possibly the number one matter that couples argue about. The inability to manage money in a relationship can give either partner a feeling of hopelessness. Unmanageable debt is the leading cause of broken marriages. Not only does money severely affect marriages, it affects non-marital relationships as well. Therefore, it is important that, while in your season of singleness, you take control of your money to avoid financial problems in the future. The following are tips that can be found in my first book, *Wealth Builders: An Economic Program For African-American Youth*, that will assist you along the way.

a) Determine Your Networth

Before you can get to where you want to go, you've got to figure out where you are. The simplest way to determine where you are is to know your net worth. Net worth is defined as the "excess of assets over liabilities." In other words, are you in debt or are you debt-free? Knowing your worth is important because it is the starting point from which you will build your wealth. If you're like most people, you're probably not too impressed with your networth. You fall into either of the two categories.

Category #1 Your current assets are greater than your current debts. Unfortunately, you were sure your assets were worth much more than that.

Category #2 Your current debts are greater than your current assets.

Right now, you're at a critical point in establishing a personal money management program that can be a firm foundation for your financial success. It's not too late to seize the opportunity to change your financial status, your current status is merely an exciting challenge. The following is a blueprint for building wealth.

b) Create A Successful Budget
A budget is the key ingredient to properly managing your money and building wealth. It helps you to determine where you should alter your spending patterns. It is important to take inventory of your finances. This means sitting down with your checkbook, entries, receipts, and credit card statements. Calculate your income versus your expenses for the past six months. Then make a list of expenses that weren't really necessary. Do you spend more than you realize on luxuries like clothes and entertainment? If so, start budgeting your money and alter your spending habits today. Otherwise you will be wondering, "Where did it all go?

The first step in the process, is to <u>Pay God & Yourself First</u>. The Bible requires that we give God the first fruits of all of our increase by paying the tithe. Tithe literally means 10%. That is all God requires. Thereafter, before anyone else gets a claim to your money, pay yourself by putting a set amount aside in a savings or investment account. Most planners encourage people to save 10% of their income. I say take it a step further. Save 25%.

Next, in order to have a complete savings program you need an emergency fund. The emergency fund should be started first. It is for unforeseen emergencies, unexpected expenses or loss of work. This fund prevents you from being financially crippled or being forced to withdraw from your long-term savings fund. Your goal should be to accumulate 3 to 6 months of monthly living expenses. Remember, it is a savings account, not a checking account.

c) Avoid The Credit Trap

With the proper use of a credit card, it can be a very important building block for financial security. With improper use, however, credit can undermine all your hopes and dreams. Just remember the following tips:

1) Choose a credit card with the best interest rate.
2) Don't borrow money unless it's absolutely necessary.
3) Set a limit to how much you can charge and don't go over it.
4) Discipline yourself so that you are always aware of how much you owe.
5) Pay your bill promptly.

d) Start An Investment Program

Investment vehicles such as stocks, mutual funds, bonds, and trusts should be considered. These vehicles are designed for long-term goals: college, a house, an education, retirement, etc. It is not advised to withdraw from these accounts. With most investments there are two basic ways to invest. Lump-Sum investing and dollar-cost averaging. Lump-sum investing can bring different results. If you place $4,000 into your fund, you run the risk that the market will fall. The market constantly has its ups and downs. It can benefit you or hurt you. Dollar-cost averaging is a process of investing money over time. You invest a set amount of money each month. With this method, you acquire more shares when the price is low and fewer when the price is higher. The result is a lower cost per share if you bought a set number of sharers each month. It keeps you from panicking when the market goes down.

As a young adult, you have a significant advantage in the world of investments. The older you are, the more sacrifice it takes to build wealth. It requires more money in a shorter period of time. On the other hand, you can invest smaller amounts of money periodically and still enjoy the days of your youth. The time to invest is right now. Wait no longer. Investing is critical to building wealth. The only obstacle that can hinder you from acquiring wealth is your procrastination.

Spiritual, personal and financial growth and development are three of the most critical stages that you must go through in order to get the most benefit out of your season of singleness. To be single and not plan an agenda is a waste of valuable time. It is important to become truly whole and complete within yourself before you seek the comfort of a companion. Whole and complete means to be full, lacking nothing. When you make the quality decision to separate and live a single life, God will fill you up and equip you with everything that you need to live a successful life. So that when it is time to meet that special person in your life, you will not operate from a position of weakness, rather a position of strength.

Black Thighs
Black Guys
&
Bedroom Lies

The Game

Meeting In My Bedroom

School Days

Somebody's Sleeping In My Bed

Whatever Happened to Black Love?

Don't Wanna Be A Playa No More

Good Lovin'

Chapter Seven

GOOD LOVIN'

Troy and Kim's relationship was no different than countless others who have vowed a life of abstinence until marriage. Formally delivered from a promiscuous lifestyle, Troy and Kim choose to re-dedicate their bodies back to God. They both sought counsel on living an abstinent life. However, their guidance was all but complete. They were instructed to be single. Yet, not taught how to live a single life. They were instructed to abstain from sex. However, weren't taught what to do when sexual urges and desires continually resurface in their lives. They were instructed to do much, yet taught very little. As a result of such incomplete teaching, Troy and Kim, like several other couples, created their own game and played by their own rules. There were no moral chaperones or spiritual guardians teaching them the dos and don'ts of proper dating. As a result, their human will to resist was constantly put on the line.

One night Troy decided to rent a movie and invite Kim over his apartment. She willingly accepted. Once cuddled on the couch in the comfort of his cozy apartment, the atmosphere was made conducive for a carnal indulgence. The movie that they began watching was now watching them. The excitement displayed on the screen was now carried out in the living room of Troy's apartment.

It all started with an innocent forehead kiss, which ended with a long awaited passionate deep-throat tongue kiss. With every meeting, came a new sexual experience. Their pleasurable kiss was soon followed by an intense exploration of each other's bodies. A snag of a bra strap and the pull of a pants zipper were the only things keeping them from enjoying the pleasures of each other's bodies. Soon, grazing and caressing each other, night after night, lost its savor. Their relationship was becoming doomed because every new experience could no longer satisfy. Something new and different had to be done. Grinding and riding each other, fully clothed, had become nothing more than a tease because their bodies were fully barracked by the garments they wore.

Sensual massages and erotic play in showers were amongst their new and favorite treats. Meticulously bathing one another's bodies. Drying each other off. Lathering with lotion and massaging one another were the closest they could get to sex without crossing the forbidden line. But their will to resist was quickly weakening. Their next daring physical encounter would be the one that would lead them into the realm of the forbidden.

It was 7 o'clock. Kim lay staring at the ceiling while outstretched on her bed, fantasizing what Troy would be like. Struggling with her spiritual obligation to remain abstinent, she settled for the next best thing. She picked up the phone and dialed Troy's number. Uncertain if he would answer, he picked up. Without hesitation Kim said, "Troy, my body's aching from a hard day of work and I need a massage. Can you come over?" Before Kim had an opportunity to think about what she had just asked, Troy quickly responded, "I'll be right there."

Though she asked for a massage, Kim desired more than a touch. What she wanted was a sensual touch, foreplay, and sex without penetration. But when Troy arrived, she got more than what she bargained for. Kim answered the door wearing a flimsy sheer pajama top and bottom with no undergarments to keep from exposing her privates. As soon as he walked in the door he very confidently said, "Take your clothes off." "What? I'm not doing that!" Kim sternly said. "Stop trippin'. You know we've already decided that we weren't gonna go there. I'm just gonna give you a massage." "You better not try anything", Kim said as he grabbed her by the hand and pulled her into the bedroom.

With absolutely no words exchanged between the two, Troy pushed Kim down on to the bed while taking her clothes off. Laying on the bed completely naked, Kim looked into Troy's eyes and calmly said, "Get the lotion." He went to the bathroom to retrieve the bottle, but came back completely naked with lotion in his hand. He climbed on top of her as he slowly lathered her body with the scented cream. After rubbing her back, waist, buttocks and thighs, he turned her over. Staring at her body, as if he were examining her, his massage quickly turned into erotic foreplay. Caressing the inner part of her thighs, Kim told him to stop. "Lay down. It's my turn", said Kim.

As Troy lay face down on the bed, Kim did the unthinkable. Preparing to lotion Troy down, she removed her cross-shaped ring from her wedding finger, signifying her marriage to God. As she lay down her ring on the nightstand, it symbolically represented her laying down her relationship with God in order to lay with another man. At that moment everything went down hill. All of the sermons, Biblical teachings and personal experiences with God took a backseat to a titillating force of passion. They began to massage each other simultaneously. In the midst of the massage, one sensual touch led to another. An oral embrace replaced the hands used to fondle each other's intimate members. But where their mouths went, their bodies soon followed. Penetration crept into their defiled bed like a thief in the night. Their extremely physical relationship had now been consummated.

Once again reliving what they both had given up, neither volunteered to end what had already begun. But as time traveled beyond the fusion of every thrust, regret began to permeate their hearts and minds. When they finally pulled away from each other, their eyes never again met. Shame had overtaken them. A sullen spirit filled the atmosphere. Once Troy left, Kim spent an hour in the tub meticulously washing her mouth, vagina and buttocks until no sign of immoral play was present. The one-hour cleansing was more than just a physical cleansing. It was also a spiritual cleansing. The act left her dirty with a stain of guilt that could not be removed with a bar of soap and water. But a spiritual cleansing had the ability to wash every sinful stain away. Kim's restless night was full of wailing tears. She knew she let God down. She let herself down. She let every person that counted on her and looked up to her down.

The next morning, Troy called as if he spent all night tussling back and forth in his bed burdened by his deliberate act of rebellion. Remorsefully apologizing to Kim, Troy swore never to compromise her relationship with God again. The sincere apology turned into a three-hour conversation full of personal confessions, tears and repentance before God. Once the conversation came to an end, so did their seven-month relationship.

They mutually concluded that their recent act of immorality hindered the purpose and plan that God had for their lives. Though they genuinely cared for one another, they knew they were being called to two different places. Sporadic calls followed until they became no more. What was once a significant part of each other's life soon became a memory of the past. A memory of "what ifs". A memory of "woulda, coulda, shoulda". A memory that often kept them in wonderment.

The story of Troy and Kim is similar to the story of millions of couples who have struggled with their personal declaration of abstinence. Leaving a world where sex is acceptable, to enter a world where it is forbidden until marriage is a major adjustment. Unfortunately, many have left the world but have taken the world's customs with them.

They have held onto the world's system of dating which says, "If it feels good, do it." It is a dating culture that is physical in nature. As a result, assumptions and unanswered questions leave couples confused. Questions like "How far is too far?" "Is sex okay if you're truly in love?" "Is it alright to have sex if you are engaged to be married?" Many who are committed to waiting never receive a clear understanding of the role love and romance have in relationships. The remainder of this book reveals specific strategies and tactics for living a sexually pure life.

Friends Before Lovers

The first and most important thing you should do before starting a relationship is establish a friendship. A non-romantic/non-sexual friendship will help you learn through conversation and time spent together who a person is. Sexual involvement, on the other hand, can shift the focus and short-circuit your relationship. If sex is introduced, physical expression can often become the primary means of communicating with one another. Your interest will be spent exploring a person's body rather than their most intimate thoughts. Sex can never maintain a relationship. In fact, sex can destroy a relationship and it often times does. A relationship based solely on physical attraction and romantic feelings will last only as long as the feelings last. However, friendship is the most important component to a lasting relationship. The premise of a relationship is "We are interested in the same things; let's enjoy these common interests together." C.S. Lewis, a Christian author, describes friendship as two people walking side by side toward a common goal. Their mutual interests bring them together.

Many couples make the mistake of entering into relationships without spending time establishing a positive friendship. They rush into romance, which often becomes very problematic. Premature romance creates a cloudy and unrealistic image of a partner. People are often seen as perfect individuals with no flaws, lacking the ability to hurt or harm anyone or anything. As couples become more familiar with each other, reality sets in. Imperfections, irritating habits and overwhelming differences that were previously overlooked or undiscovered begin to creep into the relationship. Suddenly, partners are annoyed and irritated. Criticism, snide or disparaging remarks, as well as outbursts of anger and annoyance are now directed to a partner who previously could do no wrong. Faultfinding begins and resentment builds. All of a sudden questions begin to arise. "What did I ever see in him?" "What was I thinking when I got involved with her?"

What is happening is that partner's idealized images of each other are being replaced by more realistic images. Soon the fantasy erodes. Blame will often lead to anger and either one or both partners will begin to withhold communication, love and romance. Next, the relationship is over. This sequence of events effects most relationships because they start out with the wrong focus. For too long the focus has been intimacy. And dating encourages intimacy for the sake of intimacy. Two people getting close to each other without any real intention of making a long-term commitment. There has been too much focus on romance and very little focus on friendship. The focus should be on getting to know each other not engaging in premature intimacy and emotional dependence.

In order to avoid physical and emotional intimacy in the relationship, you must pursue a Godly-based friendship. A friendship allows you to get to know a person, observe their character, and find out how you both relate as a couple. If your friend's name is Joseph, then you should become a student of Joseph by taking a class in Joseph 101. Get to know his likes and dislikes. Ask questions about his childhood days and how it was growing up. Observe how he interacts with his family and friends. Ask about his schooling. Discover his goals, dreams and passions. Most importantly, question him on his spirituality and religious affiliation.

Though you may be inclined to date a certain type of a man or woman there is no denying that one of the strongest attractions to a person is their overall similarity to you. That is why it is important to be equally yoked with your future partner. II Corinthians 6:14-17 says, *"Don't be teamed up with those who do not love the Lord, for what do the people of God have in common with the people of sin? How can light live with darkness? And what harmony can there be between Christ and the devil? How can a Christian be a partner with one who doesn't believe? And what union can there be between God's temple and idols? For you are God's temple, the home of the living God, and God has said of you,*

"I will live in them and walk among them, and I will be their God and they shall be my people. That is why the Lord has said, Leave them; separate yourselves from them; don't touch their filthy things, and I will welcome you, and be a Father to you, and you will be my sons and daughters (TLB)."

Your most fulfilling relationships are likely to be with people who share your outlooks, beliefs and values. In contrast, people who differ from your outlooks, beliefs and values don't help create fulfilling relationships. So, do opposites attract? Of course they do, but they don't usually work out in the long-term. God wants you to befriend those who have a personal relationship with Him. If you choose otherwise, it can be devastating. Their attitudes, beliefs and practices will eventually rub off on you and hinder your relationship with God. It happens time and time again. So many Christians have struggled with sexual sin and even backslid because of dealing with the wrong people.

The Bible effectively addresses this very issue in Haggai 2:12-13. *"If one carries in the skirt of his garment flesh that is holy [because it has been offered in sacrifice to God], and with his skirt or the flaps of his garment he touches bread, or pottage, or wine, or oil, or any kind of food, does what he touches become holy [dedicated to God's service exclusively]? And the priest answered, No! [Holiness is infectious.] Then said Haggai, If one who is [ceremonially] unclean because he has come in contact with a dead body should touch any of these articles of food, shall it be [ceremonially] unclean? And the priest answered, It shall be unclean. [Unholiness is infectious.] (Amplified)."*

The scripture is simply explaining what happens when you surround yourself with people who have no relationship with God. The word infectious is defined as contagious, poisonous and toxic. Therefore, if you associate with toxic people, they'll intoxicate you. For example, if you sit next to someone who is healthy you can't catch their health. But, if you sit next to someone who is diseased, you can possibly catch their disease. Holiness is something that you must choose on purpose. Being around other holy people will spiritually edify you. But, if you dwell in the presence of sinners, their sin will rub off on you. That is why it is important to be equally yoked with your partner.

Your friendship should have a spiritual foundation. The love of God must be at the center of your hearts and your friendship must be guided by God's Biblical truths. There are several things that you can do to encourage each other in your faith. An important activity to establish is the ability to pray with and for each other. I'm not talking about the kind of prayer that has you up in each other's apartment till the wee hours of the morning. To avoid any temptation, your prayer should be in church, amongst a group or on the phone.

There are other ways to grow in fellowship with one another. You can attend church service together and discuss what you've learned from the sermon. You can share what God has taught you in your individual walks with Him. You can read the bible and other Christian books together. You can also encourage and enforce spiritual development in each other. The list goes on and on. The point is to keep your friendship as pure as possible to keep any physical temptation from messing it up. This will allow your feelings and emotions to be pure and your love to be strong and guided by God.

Let's Make Love

For too long people have equated love with sex, though they are mutually exclusive. Friends, family and co-workers have often shared sexual experiences with one another using love as the premise for their interaction. You've heard it time and time again. "Remember Billy from the art department? We finally go together last night. And girl, we made love all night long." Perhaps after exclusively dating someone for a period of time, they approach you with a very heartfelt proposition. "We've known each other for some time now and I think we're ready to go to the next level in our relationship. What I'm trying to say is 'I wanna make love to you'." These are bridges that individuals often cross in their dealings with the opposite sex. Some partners cross that bridge sooner than others. Nevertheless, it is a bridge that is crossed.

Many have embraced a false definition of love. Society has convinced us that love and sex are synonymous. The *American Heritage College Dictionary* erroneously defines love as a) sexual passion b) an intimate sexual relationship or episode between lovers c) sexual intercourse d) to embrace or caress. When we look at the word sex in the same book it is defined as a) the sexual urge or instinct as it manifests itself in behavior b) sexual intercourse c) to arouse sexually. Do you see the uncanny similarity? The definitions of both words make them one in the same. According to the definitions, love is sex and sex is love. Let's think about this.

Is the motive behind a 'booty call' a desire to express love? Is a one-night stand a physical union birthed from a mutual desire to explore love? Is a partner's decision to engage in sex outside of a committed relationship a declaration of love? Certainly not! The catalyst for these sexual experiences is lust. Love has nothing to do with it. Though, many refer to their sexual partners as lover, a more accurate term is luster.

Society also uses love as a justification to engage in premarital sex. Many couples believe that once "love" is established, sexual union is permissible. They use love as an excuse for disobeying God. They contend, "We've waited a long time for this. It was really special. We love each other." For them love justifies evenings spent enjoying each other's bodies before marriage. They have violated each other's purity in the name of love. But, is that really love? In order to answer that question, it is important to understand the Bible's position on love. I Corinthians 13:4-8 says, *"Love is patient, love is kind. It does not envy, it does not boast, it is not proud. It is not rude, it is not self-seeking, it is not easily angered, and it keeps no record of wrongs. Love does not delight in evil but rejoices with the truth. It always protects, always trusts, always hopes, and always perseveres. Love never fails (NIV)."* Let's take a closer look at the scripture.

There are many characteristics. However, there are specific attributes that specifically speak to the power of abstinence. The very first characteristic of love is patience. Patience is the ability to calmly tolerate delay without complaint. It is not hasty or impulsive. Therefore, love would encourage partners to wait for the appropriate time, which is marriage, to indulge in sex. Second, love is not self-seeking. Rather, it is being sensitive to the concerns and needs of others. It does not pursue one's personal desires at the expense of another. Partners who wave the banner of divine love put aside their sexual ambitions for the spiritual benefit of another. They do not selfishly seek their own fulfillment. Third, love does not delight in evil but rejoices in the truth. Two people who really share the God-kind of love don't take pleasure in sexual immorality. Rather, they stand on the truth of God's word. It is a word that encourages people to abstain from fornication. Lastly, love always protects. If a person truly loves another, they will keep their partner's sexuality from being damaged, attacked or stolen by the lusts of their own flesh. Guarding each other's purity and refraining from sexual intimacy are acts of true love.

After truly understanding the bible's definition of love, many are left wondering what there is left to do. Many have viewed sex as the highest or only expression of love. Let me take this time to make a very bold statement. This may mess with your traditional way of thinking, however my intention is to help heal you not hurt you. Here it is. Premarital sex is never an expression of love. It is always an expression of lust. The only time sex is an expression of love is when it is performed within the confines of marriage. You may be wondering how the same physical act is honorable in one setting and dishonorable in another. It's quite simple. God said so. He has established a set of sexual laws for married couples and singles. Hebrews 13:4 says, *"Marriage is honorable in all, and the bed undefiled: but whoremongers and adulterers God will judge (KJV)."* As you can see, God declares that sex in marriage is honorable and the bed is undefiled. However, the sexually immoral person's bed is defiled. A defiled bed is filthy, dirty and corrupted by the acts performed therein. An undefiled bed is pure, wholesome and clean. Therefore, sex outside of marriage is filthy, dirty and corrupted, which is dishonorable.

But there is still hope. You can make love without ever touching another person. Love encompasses so much more than mere physical interaction. It can be expressed in several ways. The bible says that life and death are in the power of the tongue. In order for a relationship to last, you must speak life to your partner. Anytime you speak positively to someone you reinforce them.

When you speak life to a person's brokenness, insecurities, fears and frailties, you unearth the hidden treasures within them. Love your partner by assuring them of their talents and abilities. Love your partner through the expression of verbal compliments. Affirm your partner in front of others when he or she is present. Always use kind and encouraging words. Positive words are the glue that keeps a relationship together. So, make love to your partner by the use of your words.

You can express love for your partner by the things that you do. Little acts of kindness always keep the spark lit in the relationship. They may require thought, planning, time, effort and energy. But the payoff is well worth the effort. Acts like cooking a meal, running errands, making yourself available at all times are more valuable to your partner. The Apostle Paul said 'serve one another in love'. Anytime you perform acts of service for your partner you're expressing love to them.

Many people express love through the giving of gifts. Gifts don't have to be extravagant or even expensive. They can be purchased or even hand-made. It's not the gift that is important, but the thought that went behind getting the gift. A gift is something you can hold in your hand to say look I was thinking of you. It is a symbol of that thought. It is a visual symbol of love. You can express love to your partner by the giving of gifts.

You can express love for your partner by the amount of quality time that you give them. It is important to give your partner time and undivided attention. It should be time spent occupied by each other rather than the television or radio. The phone should not matter. A knock at the door shouldn't matter. The only thing that matters for that agreed period of time should be the two of you. Invest your time in quality conversation, just looking into each other's eyes and talking. Share each other's experiences, thoughts, feelings, dreams and aspirations. Experience things together. Spend time doing things that your partner likes to do. It will show your partner that you truly care. So, you can express love to your partner through the power of quality time. If you take the time to apply these acts of love to your relationship, it will restore the true love that has been missing in your relationship.

How Far Is Too Far?

How far is too far? This is a question that has been on the hearts, minds and lips of countless men and women who are considering a life of celibacy. While some view kissing, caressing and fondling as no big deal. Others feel it is completely inappropriate.

Though many couples have sworn to a life of abstinence until marriage, they have drawn a fine line as to what they will and will not do. Theoretically, it sounds like a pretty good plan. However, in all practicality, it is very problematic. You see, a sensual touch triggers a physiological response. So, while your mind tells you one thing, your body screams something entirely different. Although some men and women can successfully maintain a level of physical restraint for long periods of time, resentment, regret and guilt surmount from habitual acts of weakness, which carry them into forbidden territory.

Continuous visual rehearsals of sexual experiences make the possibility of having sex even easier. With such explicit fantasies, one thing often leads to another. Which leads to another. Which leads to another. Pretty soon, temptation arises, sin occurs and intercourse is performed. The sexual experiences, which were confined to the parameters of the mind, are thoroughly conceived. Genesis 11:6 says, "...*and now nothing will be restrained from them, which they have imagined to do.*" And to think, it can all start with a kiss.

When man and woman's lips unite, and their tongues penetrate each other's mouth, the process of becoming one has begun. Therefore, kissing is an essential aspect of the entire sexual union because once you start you crave more. Then comes a kiss on the neck, which leads to a shoulder massage. Who can forget a wet tongue in an ultra-sensitive ear that sends jolts throughout the body? Then comes the unthinkable. As he struggles to unhook the clasp of her bra from underneath her shirt, she unleashes his belt while reaching for his zipper. The next thing you know, clothes are wildly dispersed all over the room and all of their convictions are thrown right out of the window.

Well, what happened? How did this all occur? How could a tongue between his lips lead to a penis between her legs? It's simple. They were guilty of limiting sex to a simple act of penetration. They dissected the sex act into several stages in order to justify indulging in unrestrained foreplay. Sexual intimacy, including kissing, touching and penetration, should be acknowledged as a package deal. But the more any two people seek to satisfy the pleasures of their bodies, the more they cheat themselves out of a truly unique marital sexual experience. There's very little to look forward to when just about everything has been done.

Author John White clearly explains the irony of breaking the sexual experience into stages. "I know that experts used to distinguish light from heavy petting, and heavy petting from intercourse, but is there any moral difference between two naked people in bed petting to orgasm and another two having intercourse? Is the one act a fraction of an ounce less sinful than the other is? Is it perhaps more righteous to pet with clothes on? If so, which is worse, to pet with clothes off or to have intercourse with clothes on?"

Do you see how ridiculous this is? Sex is so much more than penetration. It encompasses everything from an erotic kiss, to the caress of a body part, to penetration. So, you must be aware of your sexual triggers. A sexual trigger is anything that makes a person want to have sex. You must become aware of the subtle and not-so-subtle situations, scenarios, and circumstances that turn you on. Donna Marie Williams, author of *Sensual Celibacy*, created the following Passionmeter. She powerfully argues in her book that the sexual experience cannot be broken into various stages. Rather, it is a transitional flow from one act to another. Every sexual act performed eventually carries into another once it no longer satisfies. The following is the natural course that two people take that often ends in fornication: Talking > holding hands > eye gazing > sweet talk> kissing > tongue kissing > grinding > clothes coming off > clothes off > doing the deed. For this very reason, couples should be very careful in their dealings with one another.

Much of this activity is triggered by lust, which is an internal burning desire that can never be quenched. It's similar to lighting a fire that gets hotter and hotter the more you play with it. So, unless you want to suffer third degree burns, don't play with fire. Arsonists inappropriately use matches and go around starting fires they can't put out. Though it may be cool to help ignite a flame, there are tremendous consequences to pay. You can seriously get burned. Besides, lighting fires are illegal, and if caught, can lead to jail. Well, lighting sexual fires is immoral, and if caught, can lead to severe consequences as well. The more that you can resist being physically intimate with someone, the more fulfilling your relationship will be sexually.

Establishing Proper Boundaries

The one thing that lies between you and your next forbidden sexual experience is something called temptation. Therefore, the moment you become serious about establishing proper boundaries is the moment you must also become serious about 'times of temptation.' Temptations are the entry door to your sexual downfall. Even though you may not have recognized it, you were tempted before you fell. James 1:14 says, *"But each one is tempted when he is drawn away by his own desires and enticed (NIV)."* So, the source of temptation is inside of you. This simply means that no longer can people blame 'him' or 'her' or 'it' for their indiscretions ever again. The only thing we can blame for that temptation is what lies in the lust of our hearts. Blaming external influences have always been the easy way out of personal responsibility and accountability. You've often heard things like "The devil made me do it" or "But, it was just staring me in the face. Who could resist?" They are the normal lies we tell ourselves when we want to give ourselves permission to sexually sin. We make the lies sound so logical in our mind that giving in to the temptation is the only thing to do.

Don't think for one minute that just because you don't want to fall, you won't. There will be all kind of trapdoors and moments of weakness. As soon as your back is turned. As soon as your defense is down. Bull's eye! You lust for something that you know you can not have. You handle someone else's flesh in a way that is deemed inappropriate. You break every promise that you've ever made. You deny your spirit to feed your flesh. You can't believe what you're doing and yet can't believe that you are doing it. Your worse nightmare has come true. It's subtle. It's sudden. It's all sexual sin.

Maybe it was in the back seat of a car. Perhaps, on the kitchen countertop. Possibly, on the living room couch during a movie. It could be a back street alley, in an empty classroom or hidden in bushes somewhere. Wherever your bedroom experience might have been, one thing is evident. Temptation is everywhere. It does not discriminate. It is not time conscious or appropriate. It can strike at anytime.

Everyone has certain spots on the body that are complete danger zones. Once those spots are stroked, all restraint is lost. Certain environments, atmospheres or behavior may cause someone to slip. So, it has to become everyone's responsibility to guard the sanctity of another person's sexuality. We must make the purity of others a priority. For instance, men struggle with the lust of the eyes and the flesh. Therefore, women should not wear tight or revealing clothes that will cause their minds to wander. The right outfit worn can lead a man to sex. Women wrestle with emotions. So, men should be careful with the words that they speak. Nothing should be said to stir her feelings. The right word said the right way could leave a woman naked.

Temptation must be avoided at all costs. II Timothy 2:22 says, "*Flee the evil desires of youth, and pursue righteousness, faith, love and peace, along with those who call on the Lord out of a pure heart* (NIV)." God's not impressed with your ability to stand in the face of sin. He wants you to flee from it. That means if you see any appearance of evil, turn around and run as fast as you can. Get out of there. The minute you think you can handle it, will become the very minute it will consume you. You are not strong enough to resist temptation, so stop fooling yourself. Ephesians 5:3

says, "*There must not be even a hint of sexual immorality, or of any kind of impurity* (NIV)." That means there can be no apparent indication, sign or trace of sexual immorality. To fulfill such a tall order, you must establish certain boundaries in order to accomplish this task. There are times when we must choose between what our bodies crave and what the Lord instructs us to do. If you succumb to the craving of your body, restraint may be too late. Mark Twain was correct when he said, "It's easier to stay out than to get out." So what must you do to keep from falling into sin's pit of sexual immorality?

1) Avoid Being Alone

Exclusivity has got to be the number one reason for physical intimacy. When you are alone, you will do things you wouldn't normally do in the presence of others. An empty apartment or a parked car in a dimly lit lot provides for an intimate environment where anything goes. It's a setting that allows you to relax, wind down and get too comfortable. That is why group dating and long telephone conversations are the safest forms of quality time spent. However, sometimes you may just want to be alone in the physical presence of your partner. And that's fine. When these occasions occur, time should be spent in public venues or in other places that lend no time or opportunity to physical intimacy. Focus on recreational activities. For instance, museums, arcades, plays, concerts, and church service are good places. Don't put yourself in a position where you will have to compromise your values. When, where and with whom you choose to spend your time reveals your true commitment to purity. Avoid places that encourage temptation.

2) Pure Conversation

The mind is the biggest sexual organ in the human body. Once stimulated, it has the ability to trigger physical stimulation. Therefore, it is not wise to engage in conversation with very strong or subtle sexual overtones. It is fruitless to discuss the desire to fulfill sexual cravings with one another. Especially when there is a goal to abstain for physical intimacy. It only serves to tease the mind and body. Ephesians 4:29 says, "*Watch the way you talk. Let nothing foul or dirty come out of your mouth. Say only what helps, each word a gift (The Message)."* Sexually stimulating conversation is not helpful. They plant seeds of carnality that can manifest. It is beneficial to engage in conversation of a pure nature. Talk about current affairs, like interests, spiritual topics, social issues and other neutral topics that help establish a positive relationship.

3) Regularly Rehearse the Possible Consequences of Sexual Sins
Few people ever focus on the possible consequences of their actions. They carelessly indulge in sexual activity and deal with consequences as they arise. Unfortunately, such irresponsible behavior can be both spiritually and physically devastating. Spiritually speaking, the Bible is clear in its punishment for sexual immorality. James 1:15 says, *"Then after desire (lust) has conceived, it gives birth to sin; and sin, when it is full-grown, gives birth to death (NIV)."* The death that the scripture is referring to is a spiritual death. However, as mentioned in previous chapters, sex can often lead to pregnancy, disease and physical death. By regularly rehearsing the possible consequences of sexual sin, it will help stifle physical play.

Final Thoughts

Black Thighs, Black Guys & Bedroom Lies was designed to convey a message of abstinence in a sex-crazed world. Writing this book has not been an easy task. Simply because sex has been domesticated, stripped of the promised mystery and added to the category of the merely expected. The world has turned sex into a sport to be scored and evaluated on its performance, technique and ability to reach ultimate orgasm. In fact, sex has become a substitute religion in the twenty-first century. Many have laid down their religion for a few moments of sexual pleasure. They have zealously pursued sensuality over spirituality. They have rejected their God in order to be controlled and influenced by another spirit. They have consciously replaced the Holy Spirit for the spirit of lust. Rather than seeking to satisfy their spirit, they have sought the pleasures of their flesh. The bible is clear on the results of such activity. Galatians 6:7 says, *"Do not be deceived: God cannot be mocked. A man reaps what he sows. The one who sows to please his sinful nature, from that nature will reap destruction; the one who sows to please the Spirit, from the Spirit will reap eternal life (NIV)."*

The sexual sins of this world have destroyed countless lives. Though sex is pleasurable, the drawbacks of premarital sex far out way the benefit. Divorce, unplanned pregnancy, disease, emotional anxiety, ruined reputation, resentment, mistrust, vengeance, hatred, jealously, acts of rage, malicious intent, embarrassment, poverty, addiction, a reprobate mind, paranoia, schizophrenia and poverty are all possible results of fornication. It's quit interesting how a single act of intercourse can turn a person's life completely upside down. But, what's even more interesting is how many choose to ignore the very consequences that they've seen played out in other's lives, just to partake in a moment of pleasure. So, logically speaking, fornication makes no sense. Unfortunately, sex is not a cognitive activity. If it were, many would naturally choose abstinence.

Many people believe God created man and woman and placed within them a powerful sex drive. Then He abandoned them to struggle all their lives trapped with seemingly insatiable desires which can never remain satisfied for too long. So, the physical part of a person's life can never be pleasing to God. Therefore, God must understand and overlook it since He made people the way they are. We are spiritual beings, not sexual beings. We're not at the mercy of our instincts. We have minds which means we can think. Even though our sexual urge is powerful, our minds are more powerful. Therefore, we could all logically commit to a life of abstinence. An abstinent life can be satisfying, productive, and also a joyful experience. However, committing to a life of abstinence doesn't mean that the horniness, the erotic thoughts and memories of past experiences will go away. They won't. In fact, they may intensify. One of the most challenging tests of abstinence is learning to live with erotic feelings without sexual intercourse or masturbation.

Galatians 6:9 goes on to say, *"Let us not become weary in doing good, for at the proper time we will reap a harvest if we do not give up (NIV)."* This scripture is encouraging you by saying no, no matter how hard it may get. No matter how much your body craves for what it knows it cannot have. No matter how tempted you may be. Don't get tired of doing the right thing. Don't get tired of saying no to your flesh. Don't get tired of staying in prayer. You must flee fornication and stay in prayer continuously. I emphasize the word continuously. It's not enough to do the right thing occasionally. It must be a consistent effort because consistency is the key to your spiritual success. When you consistently work towards living a sexually pure life, refusing to give up, you will reap a harvest. You will harvest a fulfilling marriage with unlimited amounts of sexual bliss.

If you have carefully read this book, you now know that the bedroom lie is that sex is an acceptable behavior outside of marriage. The truth is that it isn't. There is a tendency for some to think of sex as something degrading but it isn't. It's a magnificent and enormous privilege and because of that, the consequences of sexual sin are tremendous, strict and severe. So, purify your body, patiently wait for the appointed time and enjoy the sexual bliss within the realms of holy matrimony.

Afterward

I praise and thank God for Hasani Pettiford, whom I was introduced to by Malaney Hill, brother of Grammy Award-winning recording artist Lauryn Hill. It's been a long time since our meeting as presenters in Chicago and New York for the convening of the African-American Male Empowerment Summit. However, I have been privy to witness Hasani's growth and development. But Mississippi was the place where Pettiford peeked the interest of many, as he brought forth a subject of what now has become a full fledged literary piece entitled *Black THIGHS, Black GUYS & Bedroom LIES*.

As a writer, critical thinker and voice of those in need, Hasani Pettiford should be seen as the who, when and where, worthwhile wait of a sojourn harvest. Many books talk about what's going on, but Hasani's relationship documentary is a call to order a higher order. This book has transcended him as a gatekeeper for those striving to become whole. Writing the epitaph of a people, who have become a damaged good, Hasani has served up more than mere mouth portions of rhetorical jargon. It is more than the airing of dirty laundry. It is a call to sexual purity in the midst of a world screaming for pleasure. Hasani reveals that each reader can truly be born again despite their sinful past. This book will force people to re-evaluate themselves and it will result in changed lives.

If you take the title treaties of *Men Are From Mars and Women Are From Venus*, *What's Love Got To Do With It* and *Waiting To Exhale* and rolled them all into one, you will get *Black THIGHS, Black GUYS and Bedroom LIES*. Long after this book's release, many will have to deal with the issues written between the pages of this masterpiece.

Dr. Maurice Brian Henderson

About The Author

As a renowned professional speaker, author and television personality, Hasani Pettiford has risen to national prominence by delivering an exuberant message on success principles, wealth creation and interpersonal relationships which are as popular among college students and church organizations as they are among corporate executives. It is a message Hasani Pettiford has learned from his own life and one he is helping others apply to their lives.

In 1998, Hasani Pettiford founded his own company, *Hasani Pettiford Enterprises Inc.* The company provides instructional tapes and materials, seminars and personal/professional development programs aimed at individuals, companies and organizations. His speaking typically includes 50 keynotes a year. Hasani is a frequent contributing writer for several national publications including Black Enterprise Magazine. He also appears on radio and television interview-programs. Hasani Pettiford is one of the nation's leading authorities on understanding and teaching a prosperity consciousness, utilizing powerful delivery and newly emerging insights to teach, inspire and channel people to new levels of personal achievement which will guarantee success in all areas of life – ultimately placing success in your hands.

For booking information contact:
Renaissance Management Service
P.O. Box 548
New York, NY 10031
Phone (866) 317-5550 * Fax (212) 368-5228
www.hasani.com

Hasani Pettiford Publications
534 Mt. Pleasant Avenue, West Orange, New Jersey 07052
(973) 736-5926

www.hasani.com info@hasani.com

Item	Unit Price	Quantity	Amount
alth Builders: An Economic Program…	$10.00		$
:cess Is In Your Hands	$12.50		
ck Thighs, Black Guys & Bedroom Lies	$14.95		
		Subtotal	
	Shipping & Handling $1.50 per item		
		Total	$

ment by: ☐ Check or money order made payable to Hasani Pettiford
Credit Card ☐ Visa ☐ M/C ☐ Discover ☐ AMEX

rd # _____ Exp. Date _____

nature: _____

me: _____

dress: _____

' _____ State _____ Zip _____

Hasani Pettiford Publications
534 Mt. Pleasant Avenue, West Orange, New Jersey 07052
(973) 736-5926

www.hasani.com info@hasani.com

Item	Unit Price	Quantity	Amount
alth Builders: An Economic Program…	$10.00		$
ccess Is In Your Hands	$12.50		
ck Thighs, Black Guys & Bedroom Lies	$14.95		
		Subtotal	
	Shipping & Handling $1.50 per item		
		Total	$

yment by: ☐ Check or money order made payable to Hasani Pettiford
Credit Card ☐ Visa ☐ M/C ☐ Discover ☐ AMEX

rd # _____ Exp. Date _____

nature: _____

me: _____

dress: _____

y _____ State _____ Zip _____